Fifty Years
of
Aviation Life

Don't Let Airplane Troubles Keep You Down

David Boudreaux

PROISLE PUBLISHING

© COPYRIGHT 2024 BY DAVID BOUDREAUX

ISBN:
978-1-963735-47-5 (Paperback)
978-1-963735-83-3 (E-book)

All rights reserved. No part of this book may be reproduced or transmitted in any form or by any means, electronic or mechanical, including photocopying, recording, or by any information storage and retrieval system, without permission in writing from the copyright owner.

The views expressed in this work are solely those of the author and do not necessarily reflect the views of the publisher, and the publisher disclaims any responsibility for them.

To order additional copies of this book, contact:

Proisle Publishing Services LLC
39-67 58th Street, 1st floor
Woodside, NY 11377, USA
Phone: (+1 646-480-0129)
info@proislepublishing.com

TABLE OF CONTENTS

CHAPTER I The Aviation Maintenance Technician (AMT) —————————— 1
CHAPTER II The Aviation Gorilla ———————————————————————— 7
CHAPTER III Let Your Conscience Be Your Guide ————————————— 16
CHAPTER IV The Federal Aviation Administration Friend Or Foe ———— 22
CHAPTER V So You Want To Be An Aircraft Owner ——————————— 29
CHAPTER VI Purchasing An Aircraft for an Investment ———————— 37
CHAPTER VII The Avionics Nightmare ———————————————————— 47
CHAPTER VIII A Close Knit Community ———————————————————— 56
CHAPTER IX Running An FBO —————————————————————————— 61
CHAPTER X Making The Hard Choices ——————————————————— 73
CHAPTER XI Contract Labor ——————————————————————————— 79
CHAPTER XII Working For An Airline —————————————————————— 86
CHAPTER XIII Experience Is The Key —————————————————————— 91
CHAPTER XIV Aviation Engineers ———————————————————————— 99
CHAPTER XV Aviation Safety —————————————————————————— 105
CHAPTER XVI Aircraft Recovery Trips ———————————————————— 110
CHAPTER XVII Airplanes And Drugs Don't Mix ———————————————— 120
CHAPTER XVIII The Customer Is Always Right ———————————————— 125
CHAPTER XIX Employee Problems ——————————————————————— 131
CHAPTER XX What Can I Do On My Own Plane ——————————————— 136
CHAPTER XXI Why Do I Like General Aviaton ———————————————— 152
CHAPTER XXII Flying A Twin —————————————————————————— 157

CHAPTER I
THE AVIATION MAINTENANCE TECHNICIAN (AMT)

I'm still trying to get used to the sound of that, "Aviation Maintenance Technician". In the world that I came up in we were called A&P mechanics and before that we were A&E mechanics. A&E represented airframe and engine. Today we are still labeled airframe and power plant mechanics which is two different licenses. The airframe license which gives you the authorization from the US government to work on American registered aircraft systems. That is structural (sheet-metal), hydraulic systems, electrical systems, fuel systems, etc., basically everything except the propulsion system. Then there is the Power plant license which authorizes you to work on American aircraft engines. This includes Jet (Turbine) and reciprocating (Internal Combustion) engines. Changing the name to Aviation Maintenance Technician is the latest attempt to make aircraft (ACFT) mechanics sound more sophisticated, and therefore more expensive. I have mixed feelings about this.

First, I think it is already too expensive to maintain an ACFT, and I would like to see it more affordable for the average person. The majority of the cost is not the mechanics however; a significant part of the cost is the price of parts. Buying parts for an ACFT is like buying parts for a boat or motorcycle only more expensive. When I buy a bearing for a trailer wheel, for example, the average price is about $7.00. When I buy the same bearing for an ACFT the average price is $36.00. It may be the exact same part number. Most of the difference is due to tracking and accountability issues. An aircraft parts vender must be licensed by the government Federal Aviation Administration, Parts Manufacturing Authorization (FAA-PMA) and all the materials used to make their parts must be traceable to the original source allowing verification of quality. Parts must be distributed with an FAA form verifying authenticity and eligibility to be used on an aircraft (FAA Form 8130, or yellow tag or green tag as they are sometimes referred to). All of this paper work is what makes these parts much more expensive. By the way, boat and motorcycle parts do not require all this paper work; they just cost more because they are considered luxury items as are airplanes.

On the other hand, I do feel the ACFT mechanics should make more money. The public is willing to pay the average automobile mechanic $95.00/hr. shop rate to work on his Volvo, or Cadillac, and yet he will complain about $60.00/hr. shop rate to work on his ACFT. If your Volvo quits running on a trip the chances of losing your life because of it are slim, but if your ACFT quits your imminent demise is much more likely. Although all these rates vary with geographic location they are in this range. Personally my shop rate is on the average $15/hr. less than other general aviation shops, because I'm trying to provide a service at a reasonable price. My mechanics made $15.00 to $25.00 / hr., While Ford, and GM mechanics make $25.00 to $35.00 / hr. If you are considering an aviation career, you should know you will have to do it because you love airplanes and not for the money. Very few people get rich working on airplanes.

I started working on ACFT in November of 1975 when I went into the Air force two months after I turned 17. I had never even been close to an aircraft prior to that time, but I was mechanically inclined. My father was a jack of all trades, as they say, so I had a lot of exposure as a kid. I had done plumbing, electrical, concrete, carpentry, and mechanical work before I was a teen ager. I was one of those kids that had to know how everything worked. I can remember when I was around ten my father had me changing the brakes on neighbors' and relatives' cars by myself. If you have ever changed drum brakes on a car you know that is not exactly an easy task. My Dad used to bring old cars and trucks home and warn me, "David, it runs so don't take it apart". He used to say, "If it ain't broke, don't fix it". Today you don't find many young people who have ever taken anything apart. Most young people that I know have no interest in knowing how things work or have any desire to fix anything. If you are one of those people who enjoy fixing things, we need you in our industry.

I spent nearly nine years in the Air force and then another three years in Civil service (Civilian working for the Government). I got my A&P license while I was in the Air force in Germany in 1982. After that I went to work for Trans World Airlines (TWA) and I worked for the airline for six years. After that I moved back to the Houston area (where I grew up), and worked for Continental Express and several other ACFT companies before starting my own company (Boudreaux Aviation Services) in 2008. I ran my own company from 2008 to 2022. Since then I have been the Chief of Maintenance for a company called Hood Aero in Hood River, Oregon where I am today. I got my A&P license through OJT, or on-the-job training and taking extension courses through Embry Riddle Aeronautical University.

The process of obtaining an A&P license in itself is no easy feat.

MECHANICAL EXPERIENCE REQUIRED:

There are customarily three ways to achieve the mechanical experience required to take the FAA-required tests:

1. **Maintenance Technician School**: Attend a Federal Aviation Regulations part 147 Aviation Maintenance Technician School. Assuming the applicant pursues both Airframe and Power plant programs students will log the

required practical experience time to qualify for the tests for licensing over a one or two year time frame.

2. **(OJT) On-The-Job Experience**: You must log 18 months of supervised work to qualify to take the Airframe or Power plant licensing tests, or 30 months to take the combined A&P test. The work time must be documented and signed off by the supervising mechanic or a notarized statement from your employer.

3. **Military Work Experience**: Military service time in certain armed forces specialties, but not the training time prior to such service, can qualify a person to take the FAA Airframe and/or Power plant mechanic tests.

These schools are not FAA schools but FAA representatives have to administer the test. Personally, I think the best method is to go to work for someone and learn on the job. Not because this is the way I did it, but as I said before, you can go all the way through the school and never have the chance to experience what it is like on an actual job. Also, when someone graduates from one of these schools the mechanics out in the real world say they now have a license to learn. The reason for this is you cannot learn specifics about any particular ACFT while in a school. Two years of classes is barely enough time to familiarize you with basic ACFT structures and systems. Therefore, when you start a job you are just beginning to learn basic fundamentals and must learn the specifics for the ACFT you will be working on. All ACFT have some same basic features, true enough, but they also have many things that are type specific (Apply only to this ACFT). As it stands right now, a licensed mechanic can work on anything from a Cessna 172, to a Bell 206 helicopter, to a Boeing 747 airliner. Needless to say, each of these ACFT is very different and each takes a host of special tooling to accommodate their maintenance requirements. If you are learning on the job, not only are you learning the basic ACFT fundamentals, but you are also learning the specific job you will be doing. In the ACFT maintenance field, as in many other areas, there are so many different aspects to work in and learn. Not only in ACFT type but also specialty items. Basically, an A&P will have training in all these areas but it is difficult to maintain the required proficiency in all these areas, and so therefore, most large facilities divide these areas up. Now you have hydraulics specialist, fuel system specialist, avionics systems specialist, electrical systems specialist, and structural specialist, non-destructive testing specialist, aircraft interior specialist, quality control, line maintenance technicians, and etc. After all, let's face it; a Boeing 787 (Boeing's newest airliner) is a little much for a single do-it-all mechanic to handle by himself. If this sounds exciting to you, we need you to get in now under the current system. The FAA has been talking for several years now, about splitting the aircraft categories up by type, weight etc. Then you will have to get a separate endorsement for each category just like pilots do. I'm not saying this is a bad idea, but I would dread having to deal with getting another endorsement on my A&P license each time I change jobs, or get a new ACFT to take care of. I will tell you, over the years I have worked on so many different ACFT I have lost track. My license wouldn't fit in my wallet any more.

Now let's start this thing off right; Boudreaux had a dog named Phideaux which had a reputation for being the best duck hunting dog in the country. One day Thibadeaux came over and asked Boudreaux to go duck hunting with him and take Phideaux along. Boudreaux said, "I tink maybe dat not good idea, Phideaux not be feeling so well" but Thibadeaux insisited and so they all loaded up and headed out for the swamp. Phideaux flushed out some ducks and the shots rang out. A couple of ducks plummeted to the earth and as you would suspect one of them landed in the middle of a large body of water. Phideaux immediately headed out towards the duck and he pitter pattered on top of the water and retrieved the duck and brought it back and dropped it at their feet. Thibadeaux could not believe what he had just seen (a dog actually walking on top of the water). He thought maybe the water just wasn't as deep as it looked so he didn't say anything. A little while later Phideaux flushed out a couple more ducks, shots fired and again Phideaux pitter pattered on top of the water and retrieved the duck and returned it to Boudreaux's feet. This time Thibadeaux was positive about what he saw and couldn't keep quite so he said, "Boudreaux you told me I did not saw dat dog walk on top de water and fetch de duck". Boudreaux replied with, "Ma yea, I guarontee dat shame me somtin bad but I never could taught dat dog how to swam".

CHAPTER II
THE AVIATION GORILLA

First of all, I must admit that the gorilla thing wasn't my idea. I completed an online IA (Inspection Authorization) renewal course a couple of years ago and found, to my surprise, that this is what the writers of the course called the holders of the Inspection Authorization Certification. By the way, notice I said IA, and not AI. I have heard many people say AI but I learned a long time ago that AI meant "artificial insemination" back in my day, and more recently, "artificial intelligence". That helps me to remember that it is "IA". Anyhow, the reason they call the IA the aviation gorilla is because he is the final authority in the field. He is basically the Federal Aviation Administration's representative that is available at almost every local airport across the country. He is the only local authority that is authorized to sign off annual inspections, fill out and approve a FAA form 337, and sign off ACFT major alterations and repairs.

The reason for having annual inspections on ACFT that must be signed off by an IA is to have a second set of eyes look at every ACFT at least once a year. In General Aviation (GA) twenty-five, fifty, and 100 hour inspections can be done by any A & P mechanic. During an annual inspection the IA must be physically involved in the entire process from beginning to end. He can have assistance in removing access panels etc., but any help by owners, or A&P's must be accomplished under the IA's supervision. During the year an owner can do many tasks to his own aircraft and sign them off, and an A&P mechanic can do everyday maintenance and all inspections except the annual, or a progressive type inspection, and sign them off. It is required by the FAA that at least once a year another set of eyes has to see the entire ACFT. The IA can, however do the mechanic portion and the inspection portion of major repairs and/or alterations of ACFT and sign them off by themselves. Again, the preferred method is to have a mechanic do the work and an inspector check the work and sign it off. Most of the time this is the way it is done primarily because again, this allows two sets of eyes see the work. Secondly, due to the fact that Airframe and Power plant mechanics are much more available than inspectors. It may seem contradictory to the "two sets of eyes rule" allowing an IA to do both portions of these major items but not really, when you consider the fact that the FAA regulations are much stricter for the IA.

While the A&P does have to go through a lot of training and schooling to get his ticket, once he has it he is done, and the ticket is good for life unless somehow revoked. With the IA, he must stay current every year by completing a certain amount of training and/or completing a certain amount of major inspections or major repairs or alterations every year. Currently, he must be signed off on his certificate every other year by the FAA to remain certified. There are also a number of other qualifications an IA must meet in order to retain his certificate but my purpose here is not to deal with FAA regulations but rather explain why the IA has more privileges and responsibilities than the A&P mechanic. It might be worth mentioning though, at this point, that you are not even eligible to try to become an IA until you have had both an airframe license and a power- plant license for at least three years.

Sometimes, I myself seriously wonder if the IA certification is worth the trouble to get, first of all, and then worth the trouble to keep every year. I am far from being the smartest man who ever lived, but just so you know I did graduate from college with top honors (Suma, Cum, Lade, Valedictorian) with a Bachelor of Arts degree, and I was on the dean's list at Embry Riddle Aeronautical University where I studied for my A&P license. I said that to say this; The IA test is the hardest test I've ever taken. For those you out there who are very brilliant but have trouble taking test let me also say, I am usually very good at taking tests as well. When I was in college my nick name was "Know It All", trust me when I say this test was tough. Being an IA is mostly about knowing what the FAA regulations are. One of the reasons this test was so tough is because not only did you have to know the answers to the questions, but as I remember it, you also had to know every place in the regulations where it was written. Let me give you an example: What are the requirements for a log book entry that signs off a major inspection or repair? You would be required to not only list every item that has to be entered for this sign off to be legal, but also every regulation that deals with log book sign offs, inspection sign offs, and what is considered a major inspection or repair. You must also deal with what is required in entries for these type sign offs. This could be 15 different references and if you miss one you get the question wrong on the test. They tell me that now the test is all computerized and multiple choice and much simpler than in the old days when I took it. I don't know if that is true or not, but I do know I don't want to find out. Oh yeah, this could happen as an IA. If for some reason you fail to meet all the requirements for renewal each year your IA certification is no longer valid. In order for it to be reinstated not only do you have to re-qualify, but you must also pass the test again.

Personally, I started my own company about sixteen years ago and since then I have signed off nearly thirty annual inspections each year, so I have more than met the requirements for currency. Never-the-less, I will attend the training class anyhow for several reasons. First, technology is constantly changing as well as FAA regulations. These classes always have sessions on new technology and a FAA representative is usually always present to update everyone on changes. Just recently they changed the regulations to require the IA certificate to be endorsed every other year instead of every year and yet you as an IA still must meet the yearly requirements and maintain records of proof to that effect. If I had not gone to the training class I'm not sure how I would have found this out. Secondly, you must get an endorsement every other year anyhow, so you either have to mail your certificate to the local FSDO (Flight Standards District Office), and depend on the post office, and the government to take proper care of your certification and get it back to you safely, or take the time to go to the FSDO and hand carry it through the process. If you go to the training class the FAA usually has someone there to take care of it on the spot. You must keep in mind however, that the IA renewal can only be done during the month of March. Thirdly, It is the only time most IA's have the opportunity to get together and discuss common issues and ask questions from the FAA about current events, and do a little advertising and socializing. I have quite a few IA friends that I only see once a year. I never knew owning my own business would mean I no longer have time for anything else, but that's another chapter.

So you ask, if for some reason I was to lose my IA certification would it be worth the trouble to do it again. I must say in the position I am in I would have no choice because I am running a Fixed Base of Operations (FBO) which requires the availability of an IA. However, if I was to work for a Certified Repair Station (CRS) which does not require an IA, or find another IA to run my FBO for me, I would say no it's not worth the trouble. I guess that brings us to the next question; if you never had an IA but you now meet all the qualifications, in my opinion, is it worth the trouble? Well, that depends entirely on what your intentions are. If you want to get an IA in order to open doors for career opportunities but do not have a specific goal in mind, don't bother. If you know you want a specific job and you must have the IA in order to reach that goal, I would say you should make absolutely sure this is what you want to do and realize that this isn't just a job, it's a lifestyle. If you understand that and you are still convinced this is where you want to go with your life, then go for it. If you are considering getting the IA to start your own business then you will need it to start a FBO, but not necessarily for a CRS. So you would need to decide which option is best, or most logical for your situation.

Let me just say that not everyone is suited to run their own business, be an aircraft inspector, or even an aircraft mechanic, for that matter. I know excellent mechanics that are not suited for inspectors. I know inspectors that were great mechanics but should not be inspectors. I know great mechanics that are also good inspectors but are definitely not ready for the commitment or dedication needed to be a successful business owner. I have also known a lot of people who wasted there money going to A&P school (which is very costly) and just did not have what it takes to be good mechanics. These people have no actual exposure to being a mechanic while in school, and they find out too late that they either don't have the mechanical aptitude, or just don't like the work. People usually like what they are good at, so it boils down to mechanical aptitude. My Dad used to say, "Son, people can do anything they put their minds to". Many people who are born with that gift (which he was) also have that attitude. Unfortunately it has been my experience that this is not always true. I have learned the hard way that most things I try I can do. There are some things that I'm just not that great at. For example: I love to fly airplanes, but frankly, I'm just not that great at it. It didn't take my instructor very long to figure that out. Oh sure I can do it, and I can do a decent job at it, but it is so difficult for me that it is not fun. A good pilot can do all the things he needs to do effortlessly and simultaneously. They say women make good pilots because they are better at multitasking. I guess you could say I'm just too manly to be a great pilot, (just kidding). Most mechanics are not very efficient pilots and most pilots aren't great mechanics, but there are exceptions to every rule. When I say I love to fly airplanes, I mean if someone else does the landings and deals with the radio, and the navigation, just flying the airplane is a lot of fun. I'll give you another example: I have all the credentials necessary to do avionics installations, and I have the knowledge to do it, but honestly, I don't have the patience, I do not enjoy tedious work. On the other hand my son Steven is a self-taught avionics and electronics wiz kid. That is one of his strong points and he loves doing it, so when he did the installations, it was under my supervision and then I inspected and sign off the work. I have learned to identify my weak areas and find ways to deal with it. This doesn't make me, or you, less talented, it makes us good managers, that is, putting the best man on the job. That isn't exactly what my son Steven called it but I was the boss. No, seriously, he really enjoyed the arrangement, which re-iterates my previous statement that most people enjoy doing what they are good at. You can spend two years at A&P School and never be subjected to the atmosphere and daily pressures that a mechanic has to face. I'm not knocking A&P schools, I'm just saying before you find yourself in that position I believe it is a good idea to get some exposure to that life before you jump in with both feet. The bottom line is, I am a good mechanic, and a good inspector, and a decent business man, and I love what I do, but I know what my limitations are.

 I am not saying if something is difficult for you then you should give up. My Mom used to say to my Dad about us when we were kids, "Daddy, don't be so hard on them, they aren't like you born knowing how to do everything." What I am saying is, I have found that I can do almost anything I put my mind to and I believe you can do most anything with determination and persistence and you should finish anything you start no matter how difficult it may be. But if it never gets any easier for you and you never learn to enjoy it, you may want to consider another choice for a career. Someone once said, "If you love what you do for a living you never have to work a day in your life". Unfortunately most people hate going to work every day. I have heard some people say, "You're not supposed to like it that is why they call it work". I do not agree with that assessment. Sometimes it is because they hate the work and sometimes it's just because they are lazy. The fact is, most of the time I love going to work. You don't have to be trapped. If you don't like what you do, do something else. I used to tell people all the time, I live in Texas because I love it here, if I didn't, I would live somewhere else. I think you should feel the same way about your career choice. Many people say I'm a workaholic but if you love what you do it's not work.

Why do I love what I do? As an IA, a business owner, or a Chief of Maintenance, my job is constantly changing. I get bored easily and therefore I need to be challenged on a daily basis. An IA has constant challenges because he has to deal with the entire aircraft as whole and not just certain parts. An IA is a sheet-metal technician, a hydraulic specialist, a carpenter, a welder and pipe fitter, an electrician, an avionics specialist, a fuel systems specialist, a troubleshooter, a problem solver, and an inspector. He is the go to guy for any problem you might have with your ACFT. I enjoy being the man with the answers to the questions that my customers have. I must also say that I really enjoy watching an ACFT do what it is supposed to do when I'm finished with it. My company had a tradition that most probably do not and that is, when we finished a project on an ACFT, we all stopped what we were doing to watch it fly for the first time. I know the satisfaction it gives me to see what we have accomplished and I wanted my employees to have the same sense of satisfaction and accomplishment. I know we lost some production time when we did this, but I believe the benefits that my employees received from this tradition was worth more than what it cost.

In my company, we did all aspects of ACFT repairs, alterations, modifications, avionics, inspections, restorations, and painting but our specialty was major structural repairs and alterations. In this capacity many times we were called out to airports across the country to work on ACFT that have major structural damage or corrosion and therefore can't fly until they are repaired. Not only did this give us the opportunity to fly all over the country and see many things that most people don't get to, but it presented us with the opportunity to meet many new people and face many new challenges. If you have an airplane and fly across the country I don't have to tell you that this in itself is a worthwhile experience. I know that when I fly into these airports that they treat me like they do because they want my business. Never-the-less I like being treated like royalty, after all, who doesn't. This is sort of how people treat you when you travel across the country to fix a problem that the locals don't know how to fix. Don't get me wrong, I don't think I'm anything special; these people can do many things I can't do. If the shoe was on the other foot I would be the one treating them this way, but this is my moment to shine. Everyone wants admiration and respect, it's just something we don't talk about and never expect or ask for. (Sorry, you asked, or did you?) I'm sure you have all heard the old saying that an ex-pert, is just a little squirt out of town. If you work in a shop where they specialize in something, at the shop everyone is the same. If you take one of those people out of that shop and send him to a place where no one knows how to do what he does, now he becomes very special to them. In any case, all these things combined make my job most exciting and enjoyable. You don't have to be a business owner to enjoy these things. I did a lot of these things before I started my own company, and as the Chief of Maintenance I still do. Being an A&P, or an IA, or a sheet-metal technician, or an ACFT owner and pilot, or an avionics specialist, all has its own rewards. In several of these capacities you don't even have to be an A&P mechanic. Now being a business owner has its' own completely different set of challenges and rewards. I will discuss this in another chapter. For now let's just say, it helped to keep me from ever having a boring moment. Prior to starting my business working on airplanes was a job I loved doing, but while I was a company owner it was a way of life and all I had time for.

One day, Thibadeaux was going to the movies and when he walked up to the ticket counter he saw Boudreaux standing there waiting in line. So Thibadeaux asked him if he had heard if it was a good movie and Boudreaux told him yea, it's ok I guess and then he went on to explain how he had already seen the movie four times that day and was going back again. So Thibadeaux asked him if the movie isn't all that great why have you come back to see it so many times? Boudreaux began to describe a scene in the movie where this really hot chick was about to take off her clothes to go skinny dipping and just before she got her blouse off this train passes by and you don't get to see anything. Thibadeaux thinks about that for a second then says, "OK sha but I got to ask why you come back again if you not gonna see de girl?" Boudreax says, "I tink if I keep going to see de girl sooner or later dat train gonna be late yea"

CHAPTER III
LET YOUR CONSCIENCE BE YOUR GUIDE

THE AIRCRAFT MECHANIC'S CREED

UPON MY HONOR I swear that I shall hold in sacred trust the rights and privileges conferred upon me as a certified mechanic. Knowing full well that the safety and lives of others are dependent upon my skill and judgment, I shall never knowingly subject others to risks which I would not be willing to assume for myself, or for those dear to me.

IN DISCHARGING this trust, I pledge myself never to undertake work or approve work which I feel to be beyond the limits of my knowledge nor shall I allow any non-certified superior to persuade me to approve aircraft or equipment as airworthy against my better judgment, nor shall I permit my judgment to be influenced by money or other personal gain, nor shall I pass as airworthy, aircraft or equipment, about which I am in doubt either as a result of direct inspection or uncertainty regarding the ability of others who have worked on it to accomplish their work satisfactorily.

I REALIZE the grave responsibility which is mine as a certified airman, to exercise my judgment on the airworthiness of aircraft and equipment. I, therefore, pledge unyielding adherence to these precepts for the advancement of aviation and for the dignity of my vocation.

Jerry Lederer, Founder, Flight Safety Foundation

    I am sure many of you, as certified aircraft maintenance technicians, have probably seen this before. I could not put it in better words. As an ACFT mechanic the safety of your customers is in your hands. It is unfortunate that it would even be necessary to mention this but money rules the world. I know this will be hard for you to believe but a lot of ACFT owners are more concerned about meeting a time schedule, or saving money, than they are about their own safety. Some of them will promise to do anything, or promise to do all kinds of things for you to convince you to let something go, or turn a blind eye to something. The regulations are written for a reason. They may not always be perfectly clear, but they are written to err on the side of caution. If your gut tells you this is not right, even if it is in a shady area and the customer is trying to talk you into something, then your gut is probably right. A few years ago I agreed to do an owner assisted annual inspection on a Cessna 152. The owner wanted to do most of the work in order to save money while working under my supervision. He tried to stroke my ego by complaining about the previous inspectors he had worked with and talking about how he wanted to do things right but they were unreasonable. This was a warning sign. I tried to work with the man anyhow because another friend of mine who is a licensed A&P was helping him and I was watching and inspecting the work every step of the way. He had already gotten a ferry permit (this is permission from the FAA to fly an ACFT that is un-airworthy to a place to be repaired) to bring the ACFT to another facility to do the inspection. He didn't want to go through the process again to bring it to my facility.

The ACFT needed a lot of work and the owner promised me he would bring it to my facility to have all the work done if I would sign off the annual inspection so he could fly it legally. Let me just say here, that signing off an ACFT inspection **DOES NOT** make an ACFT safe to fly. First of all, I have no way of knowing whether he would actually bring the ACFT to me to repair or not. I'm thinking probably not or he would have brought it to me to begin with. Secondly, I would have been falsifying documents saying the ACFT met all the requirements to pass an inspection when it didn't, which is a punishable offense under the law. Thirdly, I would have been putting someone's life in jeopardy because he wanted to save money. Finally, I would have tarnished my reputation by letting someone do something that is not legal or moral. After numerous phone conversations and numerous trips to the airport where his ACFT was, it became apparent to me this fellow wasn't going to do what was necessary to make the ACFT safe. He just wanted to get a signature and get out from under the ACFT (sell it in an unsafe condition with my signature on it). He thought if he could just get a signature he could sell the airplane and it would no longer be his problem. While it is part of my job to look after the interest of my customers, more importantly, it is also my job to look out for the interest of anyone else who might fly in this ACFT. Eventually I had to tell this owner that it had become apparent to me that he didn't want to do what was required to make this ACFT safe and he couldn't buy my signature. I don't know what he ended up doing but my conscience is clear.

    I will say that most of the aircraft owners that I deal with are straight up and want their ACFT fixed properly and safe. If someone owns an ACFT simply for a toy, that is they only fly for enjoyment, they are more likely to not be that concerned about how well it is maintained. The problem is a lot of people who own aircraft did not realize how expensive they are to maintain when they bought them and now they just don't have the funds to maintain them properly. The average owner cringes at annual time every year knowing that the average cost for an annual inspection on a single engine aircraft each year is around $2500.00. The inspection is $800.00 to $1000.00 depending on the aircraft and the average amount of items that need to be repaired each year is an additional $1000.00 to $1500.00. For most people it is not practical to own an ACFT unless you have this kind of pocket change to spend on a hobby, or you can use the ACFT for a business and can legally use a large amount of the expense as a tax deduction. In either case, you still have to have the money available to properly maintain the ACFT. Even if you can legally use the tax deduction for your business that just means that the money you spend for business expenses is no longer taxable income, but you still have to spend the money.

 The other type of customer that you have to be concerned about is the business man who has a corporate jet and he makes a lot of money with his jet, or fleet of jets. Jet ACFT are very expensive to maintain, but the biggest problem is not the cost of maintenance but rather the money the ACFT is not making while it is down for maintenance. The majority of these owners will tell you anything you want to here in order to get these ACFT back in the air as quickly as possible. You as the mechanic must determine which items can be deferred (put off until a more convenient time) legally and safely. If you are a corporate jet mechanic I can guarantee sooner or later you will be put in this position. If there is an item that you think is unsafe, regardless of what another mechanic, pilot, or aircraft owner, says or thinks, you must stick by your guns. No compromise. No doubt when you are talking about jets there may be hundreds of items found during the inspection and no question there will be items that are not critical to flight operations, those are not the items I'm referring to. I'm talking about items you are not comfortable with. If you are not comfortable with an item because you just aren't sure how important it is to flight, then you should stick by your guns until you find out whether it is a safety issue or not. There is no dishonor in not knowing everything; there is dishonor in letting it go because you don't know. I will tell you that I have woke up in the middle of the night knowing that an ACFT owner was coming to pick up his ACFT in the morning and I couldn't remember whether or not I had put safety wire on a bolt that I had installed the day before. I got up in the middle of the night and called the authorities that I had to in order to gain access to the ACFT and physically went there and verified that I had done the job right and finished all the steps. So far, as it turns out, I have never found anything wrong when this has happened, but if I'm not sure I'm going to do whatever I have to in order to make sure. This is one reason why it is always a good idea to have two separate sets of eyes look at a job even if you are an inspector, but that is not always possible or practical.

Personally, I never have a problem with other mechanics looking at my work; in fact I prefer it that way. After all, I'm only human, and to err is human. I think a mechanic who doesn't want someone else to see their work has something to hide. At one time in my life I had a supervisor that just signed off work that his people did without ever looking or even having someone else look. I think that is irresponsible, and I vowed to myself before I started my own business that I would not do things that way. It is not always convenient to take the time to go look at every job, but it is the right thing to do. I feel this is right even if the mechanic is qualified to do the job and sign it off himself because everyone makes mistakes and anyone can overlook certain details. It is not a matter of trust it is a matter of responsibility. I have found that even though I can be anal about checking and rechecking, that on occasion some minor things can still get missed. The more eyes the better. It is always better to be safe than sorry. My Dad used to say, "I hope I never stop making mistakes".

There have been times when I worked for supervisors who were more meticulous than me, and I felt they were being ridiculous because the items they were concerned about were, in my opinion, not critical to safe flight. That only results in delaying the delivery of the ACFT and costing the customer more money for no apparent reason. Yet, 99% of the time I respect their opinion and do whatever is required to ease their minds. I have however, dealt with some of these situations by taking the problem to a higher authority, and on some occasions, have actually left the job. Never-the-less I cannot criticize someone for being overly cautious as this is much better than overlooking an unsafe condition. I have learned as a sheet-metal mechanic that just because a job looks good at first glance doesn't mean that it is. However if a job looks good it usually is, and if it looks bad it may be structurally sound, and it may be safe, but it is still not a good job because the customer won't be satisfied. Still I understand that if it is safe and structurally sound and time is critical and this repair is in a place where it will not be seen by the public, then it may be practical to let it go. Again, I must stress that I am talking about a repair that is legal, safe, and structurally sound, but just not as pretty as it could be. My purpose is not primarily to make it pretty; my purpose is to give my customer a good, safe, legal, job at a reasonable cost and in a reasonable amount of time. If I can make a job pretty too, then that is even better, but I will tell you straight up there are some rivets (sheet metal fasteners) you cannot get to in order to make them pretty. They will be safe and structurally sound but they won't be pretty. I'm not trying to hide ugly work I'm trying to be practical and efficient. Ok, so I'm being brutally honest, so sue me.

At Sunday School they were teaching how God created everything, including human beings.

Little Johnny seemed especially intent when they told him how Eve was created out of one of Adam's ribs. Later in the week his mother noticed him lying down as though he were ill, and she said, 'Johnny, what is the matter?' Little Johnny responded, 'I have pain in my side. I think I'm going to have a wife.

CHAPTER IV
THE FEDERAL AVIATION ADMINISTRATION FRIEND OR FOE

The Federal Aviation Administration (FAA) is the government agency that monitors all aircraft maintenance and operations in the United States of America. For the most part, I think the FAA is a very good and necessary agency. Of course it has its problems just like all government agencies. Sometimes you would swear that the right hand doesn't know what the left hand is doing. With all the hundreds and thousands of ACFT and pilots and mechanics, and aviation doctors, and air traffic controllers, and etc. to keep watch over, it is a monumental task. Many times I have felt that they seem to be harassing the little guy over trivial matters and at the same time letting many large operators get away with things they should never do, but it has to be hard. I have worked in General Aviation, Corporate Aviation, and Commercial Aviation, and it often seems that they are picking on the little guy who just works on small aircraft out in the middle of no-where. In the mean time they let the airlines do things like skip major inspections and let major discrepancies go for the sake of making money. You know the saying, "money talks". Still, I think the FAA is very essential for aircraft safety. Out here on the job, I see pilots and mechanics doing things that are not only illegal but unsafe every day. I'm not talking about making mistakes, anyone and everyone does that. I'm talking about intentional infractions. A few years ago I heard a story about a man who owns a SR20 Cirrus (a very expensive composite aircraft) and he had a blow out on the taxi way. He did not want to pay a mechanic to work on his ACFT so he and his instructor decided to fix it themselves. They jacked the wing and did not set the jack correctly and it slipped and the jack went through the bottom of the wing.

This is a very expensive goof up, but that's not the worst part. He still did not want to get a mechanic involved so he put what us mechanics call speed tape (aluminum tape) over the hole and continued to fly the airplane. If that isn't scary enough, I heard a couple of days ago this same guy is buying a jet. I am sure most of you folks out there know people who have more dollars than sense.

Another time, I was talking to a man that had his own airplane and he told me he was having trouble with his propeller governor. I told him he should take it off and send it to a prop (propeller) shop for repair. An A&P line mechanic should not work on these in the field because they have to be adjusted and set on a bench in a repair shop and then recertified. A few days later I asked him how it went with the governor and he told me, "no problem, I took it apart and put a new spring in it". So I asked him, since you're not even supposed to be in that thing, where did you get the spring? He replied that he took one out of a fountain pen. Now listen folks, a spring is not a spring. These things are manufactured and calibrated with a specific amount of force to be applied over a specific amount of travel.

About a year before that incident, I heard about a guy who brought one of my friends a Cessna 182 to do an annual inspection on. There were so many things wrong with this ACFT I could write a book about just that. The thing I want to point out is the fact that the ACFT had an O-470-R engine in it that had supposedly been converted to an O-470-50 engine. Every ACFT manufactured in the US is issued a Type Certificate Data Sheet (TCDS) which list what type of engine and what type of propeller as well as all the other critical information about the ACFT. If someone wants to make changes to an ACFT that are different than what is listed on the TCDS they must obtain authorization to do so. This is done by obtaining a Supplemental Type Certificate (STC). First of all this conversion is part of a Supplemental Type Certificate

(STC) that must be accomplished in a certified repair facility that holds the FAA certification to do it, and it wasn't. Second, this conversion requires many specific parts to be installed that are different than the original engine design, and they weren't. Thirdly, you must have another STC authorization to install it on your aircraft, and he didn't. Finally, this conversion can only be used on certain types of aircraft, and yeah you guessed it, it wasn't. It is an inspectors job to not only inspect the condition of the aircraft and engine, but also to verify that the aircraft, and the engine, and the propeller are all certified, legal and compatible with each other. I see things like this a lot. This is why we have inspections done every year by someone who is equipped with the knowledge to catch these type of errors.

I'm not trying to scare people who want to fly. A properly equipped and well maintained ACFT is one of the safest means of transportation. But I will tell you this, after some of the things I have seen I will not just jump in anybody's airplane and take off. These are some of the reasons why I think it is really important to have an agency monitoring ACFT maintenance and operations. Then every day lately it seems like we are hearing about pilot's flying after they have been drinking, or falling asleep at the controls, or playing on their laptop and overshooting their destination by hundreds of miles. Then we hear about air traffic controllers falling asleep on the job at major airports and airliners landing with no direction. I saw a safety poster once that said, "ACFT are not inherently more dangerous than other vehicles they are just less forgiving".

I have also found that the FAA can be very helpful to those who want to work with them. I have had numerous occasions where I have contacted them to get information about how to do certain types of paperwork, or how to construct a repair station manual, or find out what the requirements are to do a certain task. If you are going to operate a FBO or a CRS you must learn to stay on friendly terms with the FAA, as they will be monitoring all of your activities. It is practically impossible to stay up with the ever changing aviation industry and its' rules. If you have a CRS the FAA will assign you a primary or principal maintenance inspector (PMI) to work with you on a continual basis. He will also be the one coming to your facility and checking your paperwork and seeing how you conduct business. A lot of CRS operators dread these visits because it is a never ending task to stay on top of the daily routines that must be done to maintain proper records and meet all the FAA requirements. I'm not dissing these guys, it is a big job. This includes tracking of materials, an active drug testing program, filing 337's, proper log book entries, keeping track of inventory, and the list goes on and on. Properly maintaining and running a repair facility is a lot of work. The actual working on the aircraft is only one small part of what has to be done.

    I have also had the opportunity, and pleasure, ha, of being on the wrong side of the FAA. Several years ago I was on a major job for the Commemorative Air force (CAF). Back then it was the Confederate Air force, anyhow, we were doing a significant amount of structural work on a B-25. We rebuilt the horizontal stabilizer (that is the horizontal plane on the tail) and did a lot of other structural repairs on various parts of the fuselage (the main body of the ACFT) and wings. The only work my company did was the structural repairs. In the meantime, the CAF squadron that had the aircraft was doing a lot of other work. This Included removal of the tail section, and portions of the wings and all the flight controls, and reinstalling all of them and rigging them. The CAF is a great organization, but they would not be able to maintain these old gentle giants without a significant amount of very dedicated volunteers. I am by no means criticizing these dedicated individuals who give so much of their time and money to help keep these ACFT flying. The problem with volunteers however, is that a lot of them don't know a lot about ACFT maintenance. If you have one or two qualified mechanics and a dozen volunteers it is very difficult to see everything that everyone does. To be honest, I can't even say that it was one the volunteers that made the mistake, but it happened. When the ACFT was reassembled they flew it to an airshow in Dallas and they noticed a flutter in the elevators on the way there. The elevators are the control surfaces mounted on the back side of the horizontal stabilizer. They induce the forces allowing the ACFT to move up or down. When they inspected the tail they found one of the bolts had fallen out of the elevator trim tab. It had either never been put in, or it had not been safetied. In addition they also found a wrench still on the tail jammed between the elevator and the horizontal stabilizer. These could be deadly mistakes and therefore the FAA got involved. Keep in mind, my crew had nothing to do with the installation of these assemblies. Since there was an incident the FAA went over this ACFT with a fine tooth comb and proceeded to take action against everyone who had anything to do with it. To make a long story short, I think this was the wrong way to handle this situation.

 Personally I had to hire an aviation attorney, make numerous trips to Dallas for hearings etc., and several trips back to the ACFT to fix everything the FAA could find. In my opinion, concerning the areas my people worked on they just didn't like the way some of the rivets looked, and it was definitely not a safety of flight issue. Anyhow, on that job I had made about $7000.00 on it to begin with, but it ended up costing me close to $15,000.00, and my license was suspended for 30 days. Not to mention some irreparable damage to my reputation and my customer relationship with the CAF. The bottom line is the FAA inspectors will do whatever they have to in order to convince the attorneys that you did something wrong if you ever get on their wrong side for whatever reason. I think after a while it becomes a matter of them flexing their muscles and showing the industry who is in charge whether they are right or wrong. Honestly, I believe if you get in trouble with the FAA, whether you really did anything wrong or not, you may as well just take your medicine. The fact is, some of these aviation inspectors (not all of them) may not know a lot about particular airplanes or specific tasks that they are inspecting. If that isn't bad enough, they will be taking the case to lawyers and judges who know very little about aircraft maintenance. Basically, it is you against the government, and even though they go through the formalities to make it look fair, the fact is you are guilty before you ever show up. The best you can hope for is a bargain plea. Originally they wanted to suspend my license for 90 days, and I believe if I had not proven my case that is what they would have done. Instead they offered to reduce it to 30 days. When we had the hearing it just turned into a heated debate as to what exactly the regulations require and I got the feeling that the FAA attorney overseeing the case left there remaining unsure who was right. It is appropriate to call these Federal Aviation Regulations, (FARS) the mechanic's bible, because just like the Holy Bible, when people read it everyone walks away with a different opinion as to what it says. My only recourse was to take it to the next higher court, to another judge who knows nothing about airplanes. That would have cost me, according to my attorney, another $15,000.00 with little chance of doing any better. To sum it up, our legal system philosophy is, "innocent until proven guilty", except when dealing with government agencies. With the FAA, you are guilty unless you can prove innocence and even then you're still going to suffer the consequences. Never-the-less, I think over all the FAA is a necessary entity. Most of the operators of these FBO's and CRS's have had their disagreements with the FAA and have suffered for it in one way or another. The average person will not ever know about it. Needless to say, this is not something the average operator wants to disclose to his customers. Still, I don't hold a grudge; I think everyone involved was just trying to do their job to the best of their ability. I think the various interpretations of the regulations is another good reason to seek clarification from an IA or even the local FAA Flight Standards Districts Office (FSDO) when you are in doubt as to exactly what the regulation requirements are. Even if you think what they say doesn't seem correct, you must remember they are the authority and if you do what they say then they must assume responsibility. Therefore it may also be a good idea at times, to get that clarification in written form so you can cover your ass-ets.

A little girl, dressed in her Sunday best, was running as fast as she could, trying not to be late for Bible class.
As she ran she prayed, 'Dear Lord, please don't let me be late! Dear Lord, please don't let me be late!' While she was running and praying, she tripped on a curb and fell, getting her clothes dirty and tearing her dress.
She got up, brushed herself off, and started running again! As she ran she once again began to pray, 'Dear Lord, please don't let me be late... But please don't shove me either!'

CHAPTER V
SO YOU WANT TO BE AN AIRCRAFT OWNER

As I stated before, owning an aircraft definitely has its rewards, but it also has its drawbacks. I think anyone who is considering the possibility should be aware and informed on what is involved prior to making a purchase. If you are considering buying an airplane then you are probably either wanting to become a pilot, already are a pilot, or you have a relative or good friend that is a pilot. The reason I included that last one is because my son is my pilot and we bought our aircraft together. We both work for the same company and use the aircraft for company business as well as personal use. If you are not a pilot yet but think it would be cheaper to buy an airplane for your training than to rent one, you may be right, but not unless you buy the right one. The FAA requires at least 40 flight hours to get your license. If you rent an airplane the cheapest aircraft you can get wet (with fuel) is a Cessna 152, or a Piper Tomahawk which rents for around $100.00-$110.00/hr.

On top of that is the cost of the instructor, which can be anywhere between $25-$50/hr depending on whether you use a private individual, or one that is associated with a flight training institution. All I'm going to say about that is it is best in my opinion, to use an instructor that is recommended by another student, pilot, or friend. Most of the time pilots that are associated with a school cost more for individuals which have their own ACFT. If you use the school's airplane, then the instructor may be cheaper but usually still more expensive than a private instructor. You don't have to go to a school to find a Certified Flight Instructor (CFI). Ask another pilot that you know, go to your Local County or municipal airport and ask the attendant or look on the message boards, or look up CFI on your computer.

The most important thing here is to make sure you pick someone you are comfortable with. I have heard of instructors that panicked more than the student did. I have heard of instructors that are always grumpy and complaining and never praise. I have heard of instructors that yell at you all the time, (not good). In my opinion, the best instructor is the instructor who, never panics, never yells, has lots of praise (even for the smallest achievements on your part) and doesn't act like he is smarter than you are. Rather someone who has knowledge he enjoys sharing. I have heard it said, "The only difference between an ignorant farmer and a rocket scientist is they are educated in different areas." This type of instructor is very easy to work with and usually a little cheaper than one at an institution because he is doing it because he loves it and not because he has to do it in order to survive. Many years ago one of my instructors in A&P school explained to me that most things in life that seem complicated are just a whole lot of simple things put together. I didn't mean to get this much into the CFI thing, but if you are trying to find one it is very important.

I'm going to interrupt this topic to tell you about an incident that took place close to fifteen years ago; A 690A Rockwell Twin Turbo Commander crashed last night, (23 Nov 2011) into the Superstition Mountains just outside of Phoenix Arizona. I am telling you this because I want you to get a sense of the ACFT mechanic's life. The ACFT crashed with three adults, the pilot, a mechanic, and another pilot and his three children, ages 5-9, with no survivors. The tail Number, (Registration Number) was N690SM. (All aircraft registered in the United States have tail numbers that start with an "N"). I have worked on many of these aircraft including one with 690 in the tail number. When I heard this I immediately checked everything I could find on the internet concerning this ACFT, the crash, and the occupants. Then I checked all of my records to see if this was an ACFT that either myself, or anyone else in my company had worked on. Every time an ACFT goes down I will do this. In this case the ACFT was adding power trying to climb over the mountains and it was in the dark. At first glance, it would appear that this was probably a pilot error accident, but there will be an investigation by the National Transportation Safety Board (NTSB) and the FAA. Several years ago one of the planes that I had worked on went down due to no fault of my own and trust me you don't want to be in that position, so being in the Aviation business I want to know what happened to every ACFT that goes down. Again, I tell you this is not just a job, it is a lifestyle. By the way, the ACFT that I worked on with 690 in the tail number was N690AX. I am relieved that this was not one of the ACFT that I worked on, but it doesn't make me feel any better about what happened. Nor does it change the fact that this will probably cause ripples in the aviation industry in one way or another. Once it is determined what the cause of the crash was there will probably be changes implemented by the FAA in pilot procedures, or maintenance, or airport departure procedures. This is one of the reasons that aviation and its rules are constantly changing. Are you prepared to live this lifestyle, if not don't start.

Are you one of those people that try to identify every type of ACFT that flies over? We in the business call it the aviation fever, or the aviation bug. If you have it you won't be able to help yourself. You will be engulfed by anything you see aviation related. If you don't have it, if you aren't interested in aviation activities, if you don't have to see every airplane that flies by, if you just don't care, then you don't want to be in this business. I can tell you, it is like an addiction, either you have it or you don't. I have five sons and I can tell you from personal experience that if they have the fever you will know it from the start, and if not, then you will know that too. I have one out of five that has the fever. My other four sons couldn't care less about aviation and if that is the case they need to avoid it. If you don't love it, leave it.

Now back to the subject at hand, you are a student pilot and you are considering buying an airplane for training instead of renting one. As I mentioned, if you want an airplane just for training purposes one of the best and cheapest ACFT to operate airplanes is the Cessna 152. The Cessna is a high wing aircraft therefore making it one of the easiest airplanes to fly and one of the most forgiving. That means it is well known for its ability to recover from abnormal flight attitudes either by itself or with little effort from the pilot. It is also one of the cheapest aircraft on the market to purchase (around $30,000.00 for a used aircraft in average condition in the current market). However, the reason I said if you want it just for training is because this ACFT is very small and has a limited carrying capacity. It doesn't have a very long range (it won't go very far without stopping for fuel) and therefore, it is not a good ACFT for cross country trips. It is also not very comfortable far larger people. If you are like my son and I and weigh around 200 lbs. or more and your instructor is a fairly large individual also, the 152 is just too small to be comfortable. The low wing ACFT that falls into this same category is the Piper Tomahawk or perhaps the Cherokee 140. This is also a decent, cheap to operate and purchase aircraft that is good for training. The reason I think the Cessna is a little better is because the piper is a little less forgiving than the Cessna. With this little Piper you also have the weight carrying capacity and the range limitations. The Piper is a little roomier than the Cessna but it still can't handle the weight because of the engine horse power. The first 140's had only a 140 horse power engine and the later models have 150 hp. engines, but this is still little power when the aircraft is fully loaded and trying to take off on the short runways you will most likely be training on.

The large intercontinental airports have runways in the neighborhood of 10,000 to 12,000 feet and 75 to 100 feet wide or more but trust me when I say you do not want to be training in that atmosphere. At the smaller county, or community, or municipal airports where training is usually conducted the runways are more likely to be 1500 to 3000 feet. When you are starting your training you are not ready for short field take-offs and landings especially with an ACFT with too much weight, or not enough horse power to perform well under these conditions. If you are planning to get a low wing ACFT after you finish your training then it is a good idea to train in a low wing ACFT, otherwise I prefer a high wing because of its' stability. The reason for that is, especially during landing, these two ACFT are very different and the transition from one to another can be as difficult as learning how to land in the first place. Some people have no trouble at all with this transition but most people have a hard time with it. When you ask someone which ACFT they like the best they will tell you right away; the best ACFT is the one they fly, whatever it is. Most pilots think the best airplane is the one they have, but that is usually because either they prefer flying a high wing or low wing, or because that is what they trained in and are more comfortable in it. I will not say either one is better than the other. It depends on preference and what the ACFT is being used for. They each have advantages and disadvantages. The low wing aircraft, with the same amount of horse power is usually a little faster, therefore giving it a small range advantage as well, while the high wing is a little slower but much more stable and easy to fly. One instructor told me that flying an airplane is nothing more than a constant series of corrections. My experience has been that this true with all ACFT, but even more so with the low wing configuration.

If you are a little larger person, or want an aircraft that you can still use for trips after your training is finished then you may want to consider something different. The Cessna 172 is one of the most popular general aviation ACFT of all time. Not only is it a good efficient training ACFT, but it has the same simplicity to fly as the 152 and has a better range and carrying capacity. My son and I chose this ACFT to meet our needs. We both trained in a Cessna 172, and a Cessna 177 Cardinal, which is very similar. The Cessna 172 cruises at around 105 knots (around 120 MPH) and burns about 7.2 gallons per hour or around 15 MPG. That is about the same gas mileage I get in my truck and the plane is much faster.

We have a range of about 5 hours with a half hour reserve. That is about 600 miles before you have to stop for fuel though we never push it that far. The useful load (how much weight the airplane can carry) is about 1000 pounds. Keep in mind; you still have to subtract the weight of the fuel which is around 250 pounds. Therefore with a full load of fuel, we can carry up to 750 pounds in passengers and luggage. It is a four seat ACFT but with the weight limitation you can carry four small adults and a little luggage full of fuel, or two large adults with luggage and full of fuel. To give you an idea; when we traveled to St Louis from Texas by car it was close to 900 miles and 14 to 16 hours on the road. In our airplane the same trip by air is close to 600 miles and we can make it in four and a half to five hours. Basically, I can make the same trip in the airplane for almost the same cost and in just about half the time or less. Of course this depends largely on wind direction and other weather conditions at the time. It seems like when we travel we always have a head wind in both directions. Don't ask me how that happens. If you prefer the low wing ACFT then the Piper PA28-180 is a comparable ACFT. It will cruise at around 115 knots or 130 MPH, and carries around 1100 pounds useful load. Our 172 is 160 horse-power with 7.2 Gallons per hour (GPH) burn, while the 28-180 is 180 horse power with around 11

GPH fuel burn. The 180 is a little faster but the fuel burn is significantly higher. Both of these ACFT are good trainers that you can continue to use after your training and are fairly simple to fly. One of the reasons they are simple to fly is both are fixed gear and fixed pitch ACFT.

A fixed gear means the landing gear does not retract, it is always down. You would be surprised to find out how many ACFT land every year with the landing gear still retracted either because of a maintenance malfunction, or most of the time, because the pilot just forgot to put it down. With a fixed gear it is one less thing to deal with while training. The fixed pitch means the propeller always stays at the same pitch and therefore the ACFT is flown basically with throttle settings, while a variable pitch ACFT is flown with throttle setting, manifold pressure, and propeller pitch settings. The fixed pitch propeller equipped aircraft is much simpler for the new pilot. An ACFT with retractable gear, and a variable pitch prop, is considered a complex ACFT. These ACFT are also under 200 horse power and they respond more slowly to changes in power settings therefore allowing a trainee, or a less experienced pilot more time to react. The ACFT with engines over 200 horse power are considered high performance. Complex, high performance ACFT are generally not good trainers, but are a lot better for long trips for the experienced pilot.

I'm not going to say a whole lot about buying an ACFT if you are an experienced pilot because if you have been around ACFT for a while then you already have an idea of what you like to fly. I will say two things about this; First, don't buy an airplane you are not comfortable with. If you think you are just not comfortable with it because you have not been trained in it, or you haven't spent much time in that type ACFT, then you should delay the purchase until you get the training. I think the same thing is true for the student pilot, don't buy one till you have at least flown one of the same type. You may find you don't like to fly as much as you thought you would, or you just don't like flying that type of ACFT. Too many people buy airplanes thinking they will get comfortable with it in time and they never do. Second, always make sure you have a pre-buy inspection done. This is especially important for the first time buyer or for someone who doesn't know much about ACFT maintenance. This can be true even if you are an experienced pilot. This is not a matter to be embarrassed about. There are a lot of pilots out there that have been flying for many years that really know very little about owning a plane or maintaining one. I will tell you that just because the owner tells you the ACFT is in excellent shape and has a fresh annual (recent) doesn't mean it is a good buy. I will discuss this thoroughly in the next chapter. A few years ago I dealt with an aircraft that was sold under those conditions and the new owner is not happy. He had an annual and a pre-buy done by someone the previous owner recommended and when the aircraft was delivered it was a disaster. This is a very costly mistake.

CHAPTER VI
PURCHASING AN AIRCRAFT FOR AN INVESTMENT

If you have not dealt with ACFT before but have heard that they are a good investment. For the average person you have been seriously misled. I have heard many times, "Never buy an airplane for an investment", and I have a tendency to agree. I want to start this conversation by continuing to stress the importance of a pre-buy inspection. It is almost always better, in my opinion, to buy a used ACFT rather than a new one. You usually always get more for your money with a used ACFT. Buying a used airplane is different than buying a used car thanks to the FAA regulations. ACFT are inspected every year and are therefore generally much better maintained than other used vehicles. Far the most part the age of an ACFT is irrelevant. What is important is how well it was maintained. This is fairly easy to determine by a trained mechanic, or especially by an IA, who knows what to look for. The maintenance records are also very important and the review of these records is a significant part of a pre-buy inspection. They say an ACFT without good records is only worth half as much. This is one area where a trusting person can really be taken advantage of.

If you are looking at an ACFT which the owner tells you that he already had an annual inspection done and all is good, or he had a pre-buy done for you, you should heed this warning. Even if this owner is honest he probably had his mechanic do the inspection. His mechanic is looking out, first of all, for his customer's best interest, and not yours. Secondly, I think it is always best to have a second set of eyes look at everything since anyone can become complacent or just plain miss something. Even if his mechanic is honest and trust-worthy, if he has been maintaining this ACFT for years he may, in his opinion, feel that he knows the ACFT well enough that he doesn't need to look at everything with a lot of attention to details. A lot of times a mechanic may not consider a discrepancy on an ACFT to be important enough to mention, where-as it may be very important to you. Yes, I keep stressing honesty and trust-worthiness because there are a lot of people out there trying to make money on these old ACFT and they aren't concerned about your best interest. I have done a lot of pre-buy inspections and have run across many good deals, but I have also run across a lot of ACFT that would cost more to fix than they would ever be worth. Since there are so many people who don't know any better they can still sell these ACFT for very good money. Just because an ACFT is still flying doesn't mean it should be. Be especially leary of people who are in the business of buying and selling airplanes. I think you know where I am going with this. Used car salesmen have earned their bad reputation. I'm not saying everyone that sales ACFT are bad people but many times they may not be totally honest, after all, it is their job to sell the ACFT.

    I believe you should always have an aircraft inspected by an IA that you know and trust, or one that is recommended by a third party, before making a purchase. There are a lot of people doing pre-buy inspections out there, but this being as important as it is, I think you should use an IA that is familiar with the type of ACFT you are purchasing. As I said before, there are many types of mechanics and many types of ACFT. You do not want to hire an airline mechanic who works on Boeing 747's to do a pre-buy on a Cessna 172. Even though he may be a very good mechanic, and even someone you know and trust, that doesn't mean he knows what specialty items should be looked at on a 172. For example, the twin engine Cessna's like the Cessna 310 have some areas that are prone to corrosion such as the rear spars on the wings in front of the flaps. If you are not aware of this vulnerability that is prevalent on this particular ACFT you would never look there. There are also a lot of mechanics out there free lancing, doing pre-buy inspections, and for the most part they will just do a quick look at the books and glance at the general condition of the airplane. This type of pre-buy is cheap ($100 to $200). In some cases that may be ok, for example if you know the person you are buying the ACFT from and you already know the ACFTs' history. The problem is many times this mechanic may think this type of inspection is ok for every pre-buy and I do not agree. There is no specific set of rules from the FAA or anyone else that governs the requirements of a pre-buy inspection.

I think in most cases you probably do not know the owner, you probably have not seen the records, and you probably do not know the history of the ACFT. If that is true, then I think a pre-buy should be as extensive as an annual inspection even if the owner says it already had one. Again, you need to get an IA that you know, or one that a person you know and trust recommends, to do this inspection. Many times this is not easy to do, or convenient. It may even be a little pricey, but it could save you thousands in the long run. If you are purchasing an ACFT out of the area you live in and do not know anyone in the area the ACFT is located in, you have several options. You can have the ACFT brought to your mechanic in your town for the inspection, (which most sellers understand and or willing to accommodate). This is a good option for you because you can be there for the inspection as well. You can make arrangements with the owner to go and take your own mechanic with you to do the inspection, or just send your mechanic to where the ACFT is. You can contact a reputable maintenance shop in the area where the aircraft is located (not the same one the current owner has been using) and make arrangements with them to do a pre-buy for you. If the airplane is in good shape, this inspection will cost you around $1000.00 to $1500.00 for a single engine airplane if you do not have anything fixed there. This shop will provide you a comprehensive list on what they find wrong with the airplane. Many of the things they will find will probably be inconsequential in the decision whether to purchase or not, but I believe a comprehensive list of discrepancies is better than the unknown. The drawback is, if they find items that are grounding, they must be repaired before the airplane can fly again and then you must decide whether or not these items are a deal breaker, or if they are negotiable. But at least now, you and the current owner have level ground to deal on. If a seller does not want to work with you on this then he could very well be trying to hide something, or just simply take advantage of the fact that you don't know that much about the ACFT.

When purchasing a used ACFT there are four basic areas that are critical and are often over-looked. They are Airworthiness Directives (AD) compliance, (which I will explain in detail later), damage history, Engine Time Since Basic Overhaul (TSBOH) and Propeller TSBOH. These are areas that can significantly reduce the value of an ACFT along with incomplete records. Now you may say that sounds like a lot of money for an inspection. When you consider the fact that a used single engine ACFT in the general aviation market is going for anywhere between $30,000 and $500,000, depending on the type of ACFT, it is a drop in the bucket. Let me show you why it cost so much for this inspection. Here is an example of what is required on a typical annual inspection:

BOUDREAUX AVIATION

1. Start engine
   a. Check oil pressure

2. PRE-INSPECTION ENGINE RUN CHECKLIST
   a. Record vacuum pressure_____(if vacuum pressure is below green arc Check again with higher rpm during mag. drop checks)
   b. Monitor engine instruments (all in green) while allowing engine to warm to normal operating temperature
   c. Make sure all instruments are working properly
   d. Check mixture control
   e. Perform operational check of bendix ignition switch if installed
   f. Check all cockpit instruments, lights, radios, etc..
   g. Check all exterior lights
   h. Check Pitot heat
   i. Check stall warning
   j. Check vacuum warning light if applicable (should go out once engine starts)
   k. Check alternator light (should go out once engine is running and alt switch is on)
   l. Check alternate vacuum source if applicable
   m. Check fuel selector valve (engine runs with selector in all positions)

NOTES:_____
_____

3. Increase RPM according to POH to perform mag. checks
   a. Record left mag. drop _____
   b. Record right mag. drop_____

    c. Mag. split (Left drop - right drop)_____
    d. Carburetor heat (ensure drop in RMP)
    e. Mixture (pull until engine begins rough running then push back till smooth)
    f. Cycle propeller if applicable DO NOT EXCEED MAX. MANIFOLD PRESSURE
    g. Reduce rpm to idle

4. Perform taxi and brake checks
    a. Note any slack in steering
    b. Nose wheel shimmy
    c. Brake operation. pedals uneven, spongy, etc.

NOTES:_____

5. Remove cowlings: check for and note any oil, fuel or hydraulic leaks(engine, braking, steering, fuel system)

Additional notes/discrepancies:_____

BOUDREAUX AVIATION
ANNUAL INSPECTION REQUIREMENTS

Required documents:
aircraft registration, airworthiness certificate, most recent AD compliance record, aircraft log books, current weight and balance, STC's, 337's, current tach/hobbs time, and equipment list giving make, model/part number, serial number of listed items.

Items required on equipment list:
Left and right magnetos, electrical and mechanical fuel pumps if applicable, ELT (showing battery replacement date), vacuum pump, oil cooler if applicable, carburetor/throttle valve, alternator, starter, all vacuum filters and induction filter (P/N's and last replacement dates), oil filter, fuel injection system distribution valve(if applicable), propeller governor if applicable, type and quantity of oil.

Note: for any other parts that will require replacement during inspection (hardware, brake parts, etc..) log the make, P/N, serial number and nomenclature of both the old part and the replacement part.

Inspection:
1. Accomplish Boudreaux Aviation Pre-inspection engine run checklist.
2. Remove engine cowlings and perform compression test and drain oil with engine still hot. Record compression test results below.

Compression test results: _____

3. Open oil filter and inspect for metal or send sample for inspection.
4. Replace oil and filter.
5. Remove spark plugs, clean, gap, test, rotate, and re-install or replace as needed.
6. Check magneto timing.

7. Remove battery, service and charge as necessary. Check battery tray for corrosion, cracks, etc…
8. Open all access panels, cowlings, fairings, leg fairings, wheel pants, prop spinner, wing tips, horizontal stabilizer tips(if removable), and interior for inspection (do not open fuel tanks).
9. If aircraft has retractable gear it must be placed on jacks and have extension/retraction normal and emergency checks.
10. All aircraft equipped with transponder and altitude encoder are required to be re-certified every 24 months.
11. Remove wheels and bearings. Clean, inspect bearings and races (replacing if necessary), re-pack and re-install bearings. Inspect brakes and calipers for wear and leaks. Service reservoir/s as needed and bleed if necessary. Re-install wheels and brakes.
12. Check/replace vacuum and induction filters as required. (usually 100hrs or annually)
13. Remove fuel strainer, clean and re-install.
14. Accomplish any new and repetitive Airworthiness Directives that are due.
15. Check struts for proper servicing.
16. Lubricate all flight control pulleys, rodends, bellcranks, and hinges, gear linkages, and eng controls
17. Lubricate constant speed prop if installed according to manufacturer's recommendation. Normally aeroshell 6. Inspect for scratches, dings, nicks, wear, and leaks.
18. Remove, inspect, clean and re-install injectors with new o-rings if applicable.
19. Check all flight controls and engine controls for proper rigging, cable tensions and control travel.
20. Perform visual inspection of all aircraft systems.
21. Wash engine and perform post inspection engine run for leak and operational checks.

After all inspections are completed, ADs are complied with, and repairs completed, re-install access panels, fairings, interior, etc...

These checklists are my own creations and are designed for single, reciprocating engine aircraft only. Twin engine ACFT and Jet ACFT are whole other story. There are also check list sometimes available in the individual ACFT service manuals and the FAA, Advisory Circulars such as AC43.13-1b. So you see, an annual inspection is a very extensive and detailed look at the entire ACFT and can be very time consuming if done properly. It will leave no doubt as to what kind of condition the ACFT is in. To sum it up, yes an experienced ACFT dealer, or an experienced ACFT mechanic can purchase an ACFT for an investment. He can either do the inspections and maintenance himself, or have it done at a reasonable rate by prior arrangement and still be able to make a profit. For most people however, it is not cost effective or practical to invest in an ACFT as it usually cost as much to have it repaired as what you will make off of it in the end.

One last thing I want to mention here, and that is considering the purchase of an experimental ACFT. You must understand that an experimental ACFT is not the same as a manufactured ACFT. You do not have to be an ACFT mechanic to purchase, build, or maintain an experimental ACFT. This ACFT has limitations that a typical manufactured ACFT does not. Experimental ACFT are restricted in the type of airspace they can be flown in, and cannot be used for any type of commercial use. Many of these ACFT are purchased by non-mechanics and are built in their garage. Many of these ACFT have never been looked at by a licensed mechanic. A lot of the people who build these ACFT are experienced mechanics, and their ACFT are just as good as the manufactured ACFT, but many or not. Since these ACFT can be maintained by their owners, with little or no rules to follow, and no input from trained, licensed mechanics, I am personally a bit leary. Many of these owners go above what the FAA requires and have their experimental ACFT inspected by an IA every year just like other owners, and keep records just as well also. On the other hand many don't, and I have seen some owners do things they could never do on a manufactured ACFT. If these guys use a spring from a fountain pen to fix their propeller governor no-one will ever know. The whole idea is that these guys are not allowed to let passengers fly except at their own risk, and these ACFT cannot be flown in populated areas, so they are only putting themselves at risk. It is sort of like, in many states, you don't have to wear a helmet on a motorcycle because you are only putting yourself and those who accept the risk in danger. For this reason I don't think purchasing one of these ACFT is a good idea unless you know and understand the circumstances.

CHAPTER VII
THE AVIONICS NIGHTMARE

The avionics nightmare, in general aviation at least, is a multifold problem. Some of this is self-imposed for many ACFT owners. There are so many different products available out there that sometimes, it is difficult to choose what you want to have installed in your airplane. Then there is the problem of choosing who you would like to have to do the installation. Sounds simple doesn't it, not at all. Then perhaps the worst part is how much can you afford, or is it practical. Avionics equipment is completely out of reach for most owners and yet the government continues to mandate updates. In the beginning things were so much simpler. You had your basic engine instruments including, oil pressure indicator, engine temperature, a tachometer, and maybe a fuel quantity indicator. Then you had your avionics package including an air speed indicator, an altimeter to tell you the altitude you were flying at, and a magnetic compass displaying the heading or direction of flight. The well-equipped ACFT also had an attitude indicator which shows the pilot if he is flying strait and level or upside down etc. In the old days that was all you needed to be safe. There was very little traffic in the air. There were also no major airports requiring modern ACFT to have extremely accurate instruments that show their position in relation to the airport and other traffic. Now your basic engine instruments for a reciprocating engine (piston engine) ACFT include: oil pressure, oil temperature, tachometer, cylinder head temperature (CHT), exhaust gas temperature (EGT), manifold pressure, vacuum pressure, fuel flow and fuel quantity. Even though basic engine designs for general aviation ACFT have not changed much since the 1940's, many of these instruments were added to help monitor engine operating parameters therefore extending engine life. Modern

ACFT engines are very reliable and are designed in a way that even if they have a failure it is unlikely that they will stop running altogether. There is a lot I could tell you about ACFT engines but that is another topic in itself. As for the modern day avionics package, this is where it gets more complicated. After the days of only having the basic necessary flight instruments aviation upgraded to what is now known as the six-pack. This included:

An airspeed indicator – Indicates the speed at which the ACFT is traveling through the air around it. Indicated airspeed is not the same as ground speed or true air speed.

An attitude indicator – Indicates the attitude of the ACFT in relation to the ground. (Strait and level flight, upside down etc.)

An altimeter – Indicates the altitude of the ACFT above sea level based on barometric pressure outside the ACFT. This is not the altitude above the ground and must be corrected for other than standard conditions. Standard pressure is 29.92 inches at sea level and 69 degrees Fahrenheit.

A vertical speed indicator – The VSI indicates the rate at which the ACFT is climbing (gaining altitude) or descending (losing altitude). This value is indicated in feet per minute.

A heading indicator – Indicates the horizontal direction that the nose of the ACFT is pointing. This may or may not be the true direction the ACFT is traveling which changes with wind speed and direction.

A turn coordinator – Indicates the ACFT attitude, as well as the coordination between the ailerons and the rudder in a turn.

These are the standard flight instruments that came as standard equipment in all of the manufactured ACFT in the US since the 1950's. To learn more about these instruments and their functions look on the web. Under http://www.learntofly.ca/six-pack-primary-flightinstruments.

Today the newest ACFT still have the same instruments but they are now part of a glass cockpit display known as a multiple function display (MFD). This is an electronic display that combines all of these instruments in one display unit similar to an I-pad built into the ACFT instrument panel. Some people do not consider this display part of avionics as the term avionics generally refers to navigational equipment. Since the term avionics is a combination of aviation and electronics I believe the new electronic display of the primary flight instruments would fall into this category as well.

For the Wright brothers navigation and communication equipment consisted of a hand held radio and a map. Visual flight was mostly accomplished by following the roads or other known land marks. This is referred to as flying visual flight rules or VFR. Back then there was no electronic flight aids. Now, almost all ACFT have at least one very high frequency (VHF) radio, most have two, and some have three. That part is easy, when we discuss navigation, that is a different story altogether. Navigation is basically using whatever aids are available to figure out where you are and where you are going. Like I said before, basic navigation back in the day was following a map, and using what was basically a slide rule. It was for figuring out what affect the wind speed and direction was having on your airspeed indicator and indicated heading. When I was a kid my Dad, my four brothers, and I, used to go fishing and hunting practically every week end. It is very easy to get lost in the woods, or on a large lake, or especially in the Gulf of Mexico. My Dad was one of those people who could go out in the woods or one of those other places without any navigational aids at all, and find his way back effortlessly. He always knew which direction home was. He said he could smell Mom's cooking twenty miles away, yea right. When you have the ability to do this in an ACFT it is referred to as flying by the seat of your pants. There used to be many pilots who had this natural ability but I think that is a thing of the past. Several different navigational aids have been introduced since then, many of which are now either obsolete or are currently in the process of being phased out. Some of these systems are ADF, which was basically a radio receiver that would tune in to your local AM radio station and use an indicator to point in the direction the signal was being transmitted from. Some ACFT still have these systems installed but they are usually just used to listen to the radio or not at all. The problem with this system was it pointed you to the radio station, not the airport. While it may get you in the vicinity of some major cities, most airports were not in the major cities. Like my old Dad used to say, "Close but no cigar". Another system that has been phased out is the Loran system. This system used fixed radio transmitters located across the country that were received in the ACFT by a Loran receiver. This receiver had to receive signals from three different transmitters to triangulate your position globally. The problem with this system was the fact that you had to have three signals for it to work. The task of keeping up so many transmitters across the country was extremely difficult. As a result, the majority of the time the system was useless. With both of these systems the range at which the system functioned was extremely limited. You would have to fly by the seat of your pants or with a magnetic compass (which is not very accurate for long distances) until you were close enough to your destination for the radio signals to function. The Loran transmitters are no longer functional and though some ACFT still have these receivers installed they have no function. The Loran system was more-or-less replaced by the VOR beacons and receivers. The VOR works very much like the Loran did except the VOR beacons transmit in 360 degree radials. The receiver in the ACFT can lock onto one of these radials and you can track to or from the radials to follow previously established routes or to go directly to or from airports with VOR transmitters.

This system has more range and requires one third the up keep of the Loran system because you only need one signal for the system to work. You can also still use the VOR to triangulate the same way you did the Loran but your ACFT has to be equipped with multiple receivers for it to work in that capacity. Almost all ACFT today have two VOR receivers and many will have three. Having two VOR receivers serves as a great back up because you can track your ACFT leaving an airport on one radial while tracking your ACFT going to another airport on the other. With one receiver you can track to or from but not both at the same time. Today when someone says they have a Nav/Com radio, they are saying they have a radio that can receive a VHF (communication) signal and a VOR (navigational) signal in the same unit. This is the system that is still most commonly used in general aviation ACFT today. This system incorporates a navigational receiver indicator that has a "to and from" indicator as well as a needle which points to the radial that the signal is being received from. This indicator is called a course deviation indicator or a CDI. It is called a CDI because this indicator points in the direction that you should travel in to reach your destination which deviates from your heading indicator that shows the direction the nose of the ACFT is pointing in. If there is no wind there will be no course deviation, but that is not likely. Your true heading is the direction the ACFT is actually traveling in, which most of the time will be different than the heading indicator and the CDI. Your track is the direction your ACFT has already traveled in. Confused yet?

    OK, now that you are thoroughly lost, I will tell you that the VOR system will soon be phased out as well. The newest, easiest, and most accurate means of navigation today is the GPS, or Global Positioning Satellite system. All of the new ACFT are being delivered with GPS receivers. The VOR system is still being used as a back-up system for when the satellite signal fails. If you go take a flight check ride, (Pilots all have to have their licenses revalidated every two years by an instructor to remain current), most of the flight examiners will still want to see you use the VOR. This is because even though the GPS is much more accurate it is not always available. Satellite signals can be affected by weather and sometimes satellites are unavailable for one reason or another and therefore not 100% reliable. I have told you all this to explain that the new MFD's or cockpit I-pads incorporate the VHF radio, the VOR radio, the GPS receiver, and the CDI all into one unit. This same unit may also be able to display all or some of the flight instruments, and all or some of the engine monitoring instruments. Each avionics manufacturer builds these displays differently, and they will provide different combinations of units to access numerous and various possibilities in displays. In addition there are several other functions that can be incorporated into these units such as: Traffic Collision Avoidance System (TCAS), Wind shear alert systems, Terminal area traffic systems, The audio panel (which allows you to select what radios you want to listen to or talk on etc.), the transponder, which transmits information such as your position and altitude to the control tower, terrain alert systems, and ground proximity alert systems.

It is too complicated to go into which companies sell what equipment and what it all does but here are some of the most commonly used manufacturers that or used in general aviation: Garmin, Avidyne Preferred, Bendix/King, or Honneywell, and Aspen. As for the cost of these upgrades, I will give you an example. A few years ago we installed a Garmin audio panel, a Garmin transponder, and a Garmin GNS 430W, which incorporates a GPS/NAV/COM receiver all in one, with all the associated antennas in a Cessna 172. The cost was between $25,000.00 and $30,000.00. Let it suffice to say, that you can easily have as much money, or more, invested in avionics as you do in your ACFT. On top of that, we installed these units one year and about a year later most of them were already discontinued or have up-grades available.

The last area concerning avionics that I want to briefly touch on is choosing a shop to install your avionics. There is no shortage of avionics shops. Off the top of my head I could list at least seven shops in the area that can do this type work, not counting my own. Each of these has its advantages and disadvantages but almost without fail, I have either seen some substandard work first hand, or I have heard through the grape-vine about some of the problems that have been associated with these installations. I find it hard to believe that this problem is limited to one geographic location. There was one installation that I was involved in not too long ago that I will use for an example. I was only involved in this installation, in that my company was hired to do the sheet metal part. That is the installation of avionics racks, installing antennas, installing bulkhead feed through fittings, and modifying the instrument panel to accommodate the control units. To start with, an independent avionics contractor was hired to install the separate units in the system and do all the wiring. After spending about three months on the job, thinking it was all ready to go, when it came time to do the operational checks the system didn't work. He spent about another month trying to troubleshoot the system to find out what was wrong. Finally the customer was fed up and decided to fire him and hire another company to finish the job. The second company said the whole installation was wrong and they took everything out and started all over. They finally got everything rewired and working after about another three weeks and another excessive amount of money. The ACFT left the facility and went back home. The customer continued to have problems with the system and this new company flew to the ACFT home base several times to try to get everything working to the customer's satisfaction but it never happened. Finally, the customer hired another avionics shop to come in and go through the system again. The new company found that this system was supposed to be installed with a built in back-up system in which a number of the input signals were switched to another source. As it turns out none of the back-up sources were ever tied into the system and therefore whenever you tried to use the alternate system nothing worked. This is just one example, I could give many more but I have seen avionics installations that were not only wrong but even dangerous and many of these were done by reputable shops. I understand that these installations can be very pain-staking, and time consuming, but there is no excuse, in my opinion, for not following the installation instructions. These people are supposed to be specialists in their area and ACFT owners trust them with their lives.

We had one customer that was complaining about static in his radio. So we thought it might be a loose connection or a bad ground. He had just had an annual inspection done, and just before that he had some avionics work done at a local avionics shop. When we looked under the instrument panel to see if we could find the problem we noticed that the new wire bundle was hanging down into the elevator control mechanisms. Every time he pulled back on the control wheel it would hook onto the wire bundle and pull all the wires back about six inches. Not only was this pulling all of the wires loose for the avionics, but the elevator travel was severely restricted. This is dangerous because as long as the ACFT remains in normal operating ranges the travel was enough to accommodate however, if he had ever gotten into a position where he needed full elevator deflection it would not have been possible. Everyone makes mistakes, but this is why every job needs to be looked at by more than one person. It is possible that this could have been missed by the technician doing the installation. It should have been found however, when the work was inspected after the installation was completed. On top of that, one of the things that should be checked during an annual inspection is flight control travel and it apparently was not. All I can say is use a reputable shop for your installations and then when you get your airplane home have your own mechanic take a second look. It is always better to be safe than sorry and if you do not have a licensed A&P mechanic that you can trust taking care of your airplane, then maybe you should.

Way down in Louisiana, Boudreaux's old lady had been pregnant for some time and now the time had come. So he brought her to the doctor and the Doctor began to deliver the baby. She had a little boy and the doctor looked over at Boudreaux and said, "Hey, Boudreaux, you just had you-sef a son! Ain't dat grand! Boudreaux got excited by dis, but just then the doctor spoke up and said, "Hold on! We ain't finished yet!" The doctor then delivered a little girl. He said, "Hey, Boudreaux, you got you-sef a daughter too! She a pretty lil ting." Boudreaux got kind of puzzled by this and then the doctor said, "Hold on, we still ain't got done yet!" The doctor then delivered another boy and said, "Boudreaux, you just had you-sef another boy!" When Boudreaux and his wife went home with their 3 children, he sat down with his wife and said, "Mama, you remember dat night what we run out of Vaseline and we had to use dat dere Tree-in-One Oil?" His wife said, "Yeah, I do!" Boudreaux said, "Man, it's a darn good ting we didn't use no WD-Forty."

CHAPTER VIII
A CLOSE KNIT COMMUNITY

I want to spend some time now talking about some very positive things. The aviation industry is an extremely close nit community. While at times this can be a bit discouraging for some businesses because if you make a mistake it won't be long till everyone in the industry knows about it. But it also helps keep everyone honest. For the most part, the people I have met in this business are very honest and conscientious. The world is a cruel place these days, especially since the economy has gone down the drain. Every day you here about stealing and cheating and people who are taking advantage of one another. There is not a whole lot of that in our industry. Most of the aviation companies that I deal with all have a great deal of respect for one another. I hope you have noticed that I have not mentioned any names as I tell you these stories about things I have seen. I do not believe that these people are intentionally trying to do substandard work, or sabotage any ones ACFT, or cause anyone any bodily harm. We are all just trying to make an honest living by providing a service to our customers that is safe, reliable, and cost effective. Now I would like to point out some names of companies and individuals that I would recommend. Not because they have never made any mistakes, but rather because I know they are good honest respectable companies that I trust. First, there is George Ham the owner of air weight Inc. in Houston Texas. I consider George a good friend who has gone out of his way to help me when I first started my company. He is the former owner of Ham Aviation which was located at Hobby airport in Houston Texas. George recently closed Ham Aviation and started running Air Weight Inc. full time mostly due to health issues. Sometimes other companies will spread rumors in order to eliminate competition and take your customers.

George is not one who will participate in this type of activity. Another is the FBO at Houston Executive Airport in Brookshire Texas just outside of Houston. The director of maintenance (DOM) there is Scott Caggiano. Scott is a good honest mechanic who will do whatever he has to in order to provide you a good quality service. I consider Scott a good friend and a man of his word. Another is Global Aviation Services Inc. at Bush Intercontinental airport in Houston. Global Aviation is owned by a good friend of mine named Douglass Ray. Global is a certified repair station that services Twin Commanders, Lear jets, Falcon jets, Citations, and Hawkers. Global has a good reputation in the industry and they provide a quality service to their customers at a rate that is comparable to any other repair station providing the same services. Another is Bill Wynn who is an independent mechanic that now works at a facility with his son in Pearland Texas at Pearland Regional airport. Bill is probably one of the nicest, fairest, most easy going individuals I have known in the industry. Bill used to own and operate an FBO at Scholes Field in Galveston Texas where he had a great reputation and a significant customer base that depended on him. He lost almost everything he had when Hurricane Ike came through so now he works out of a hanger in Pearland. Another is Brad Crudup, who used to be the Director of Maintenance (DOM) at Global but is now working overseas. Brad is probably one of the best A&P mechanics I have ever met. He knows the Twin Commander better than anyone else I know. He is also just a good, fair, honest person. Another is Tom Foreman who is an aircraft owner and operator and runs the airport terminal facility at the Orange County airport in Orange Texas. Tom is just a great guy that is very kind and helpful to everyone. He owns a V35 Beech Bonanza and is one of my customers. Another is Rite-way Aviation located at Hooks airport in Tomball Texas. They are a certified repair station and a Cessna parts distributor.

If you ever need work done on your Cessna at Hooks airport, or just need parts, call and ask for John or Donna. They are very helpful, kind, and accommodating. Another is Texas Turbine and Prop., owned by Joe Washburn. Joe specializes in King Air maintenance and is dedicated to providing his customers with the best maintenance available. Joe has always been willing to help me out with information or advice and I have done several sheet metal jobs for his company. Joe also helped me out when I started my company when many others were too worried about competition. This list could go on and on but I think you get my point. The Aviation industry is filled with good, honest, people who are just trying to make a living and they won't treat you like you are just a number. It has been several years now since I have dealt with some of these vendors and I know some of them are no longer in business, however I still believe they have earned a favorable mention.

 I would also like to say here that in general aviation I have the opportunity to serve some of the best people I have ever had the privilege of knowing. Most private ACFT owners are just plain good folks. There are people who will try to take advantage of you in any industry. In General aviation however, my experience has been that the majority of the people I deal with are loyal, reliable, and honest customers. Again, I can't mention everyone here who has helped to make my business successful and I will probably forget to mention some. I am not in this business to get rich. I want to help these people to enjoy flying safely and I hate to see an aircraft just sit idle and fall apart. There are aircraft bone yards all over this country were once good airplanes are just sitting there falling apart because a flight school or some other aviation business failed and the owner refuses to lose money on these aircraft. Therefore they just sit there until they fall apart. What a waste, it makes me sick. Principal is more important than money. That is why I will never be wealthy but at least I can sleep at night. I think of myself as being dedicated to the man and the machine. There have been numerous times when I have paid for repairs out of my pocket in order to get an aircraft back in the air. There have been a few times when I never got my money back, but someone told me a long time ago that anytime you help someone it will cost you something. This is just something you have to accept. It helps me feel good about who I am. I must say that these folks are not just my customers, they are my friends. Unfortunately, I have known several people in the industry that respond to that by saying, "customers should never be considered friends, they are customers and I provide them a service for a price and that's that". I may not be a good business man with my attitude, but for me, it's more about doing the right thing than making money. Anyhow, some of the customers that I would like to thank for being loyal customers and good friends are: Ron Huebel, Lonnie Cavel, Lee Rector, James Flemming, Wilbur Hah, Richard Turkel, Larry Webb, John Neff, Robert Smith, Bob Wymert, Jeff Loomis, Jose Damas, Jonathon Jackson, Ace Thomas, Steve Taylor, Carey Burmingham, L-3 Vertex, DS-2, Coy Elliot, Dan Barclay, David Dubose, Doug Manning, Garrick Androl, Jody Schupe, Jason Bolz, Orange County and Chambers County Mesquito Control, John Horner, Beth Jenkins, Wally Warren, as well as the others I have already mentioned, and who knows how many others I have forgotten. Thank you all for your business, your trust, and your friendship. You are part of the reason I love what I do.

    Some of the other reasons I love what I do is because of the fellow mechanics and employees and others who have supported me. Back then I did own the business, but my employees were my fellow workers. I'm not the type to sit in my office and give orders. Some of my past employees were: Steven Boudreaux (My son and my right hand man), Steve Jeanes, Marty and Joshua Hatley, Richard and Pam

Palmer, Rose Baxter (My sister who runs her own business and has been a tremendous help to me), John and Richard Boudreaux (My brothers who have also been financially and physically supportive), Rachel Boudreaux (My daughter-in-law who became my administrator), Ricky Terry, Henry Boudreaux (My cousin who has been a part time employee and helped to provide various pieces of equipment and advice). Today is Thanks Giving Day, how appropriate. I also get the opportunity to work with a great host of suppliers that I have dealt with for years now like; Falcon Crest Aviation, Hatfield Aviation, Clem's A&E Service, Rite-way Aviation, Aviall, and Aircraft Spruce. You guys make it possible, Thanks. Aviation folks are a close nit bunch. I like to think of us as one big happy family. As a traveling mechanic many times we fly off in our plane to go help one of our customers stranded somewhere. Sometimes our plane isn't available for one reason or another. Every one of those guys I mentioned earlier either will, or already has flown with me to go help someone else and either stayed there with me till I got the problem fixed, or flown me and the stranded customer back home free of charge. They won't even let me pay them for the gas. They always say, "It could be me next time". They are right, it could be, but come on, it's more than that, and we are all in this together. Since my move to Hood River Oregon, I miss all my former colleagues, but I am currently developing the same type of comradery with a new host of customers and co-workers.

CHAPTER IX
RUNNING AN FBO

    I am calling this chapter "running a FBO" but it could just as well have been called running a business. Some of this conversation will be aviation specific for sure, but I think the majority of what it takes to run a business can apply to any business in the US. I sincerely hope these morsels of advice will be helpful to anyone in aviation or considering getting in. Let me start by saying, it is very difficult to just move into a town and start a business. I know I could not have done that, I had to know a lot of people in the business where I started for it to work. When I first began there were few customers who knew me other than those who were customers of my previous employer. I did not want to take any of his customers so I had to try to find my own customers which would have been impossible without contacts. I have known many business people who started by taking all of their previous employer's customers. I believe that is wrong. Eventually I did end up getting some of those customers but I did not contact them. After they found out I started my own business they contacted me. I have tried all my life to avoid burning bridges between myself and others I have worked for, but sometimes it is unavoidable. When I left my previous place of employment I had worked there for almost six years and we were good friends. When I left there I guess they felt betrayed. We have not spoken since and have broken all ties. If they read this someday I want them to know that this is not what I wanted and even though the opportunity presents itself more often than you would think, I have never spoken ill of them to anyone. I won't mention any names here, but you know who you are. There have been a number of attacks against me for various reasons but I make it a policy, to not do that to anyone. I'm sure you have all heard, "If you don't have anything good to say about someone, don't say anything". I believe you can always find something good to say anyhow. For some reason mechanics are very critical of one another and I have to work hard at not being that way. I think it is a good practice to not bad mouth folks, I do not wish any of these people any harm or bad luck. I think there is plenty of work to go around. I want to share with you a letter I wrote recently involving an incident with an avionics shop, but keep in mind no-one knows about this except the people directly involved and I have every intention of keeping it that way:

It is with great sadness that I have to write this letter as I feel you have done XXXXXXXXX, Me, and yourself a grave injustice. I will not take the time here to go back over all of the wrong that you have committed, I feel confident that after reading my last letter you know how I feel. The bottom line is you started a job after you quoted a certain price, told the customer that a part could not be adjusted and would have to be replaced (when in fact it could be adjusted and eventually was by someone else), did a partial inspection that you promised to send paperwork for and never did, promised to finish the inspection at no extra charge and now refuse to, and now you are sending a bill for 50% more than the original quote for a job never done. I realize that it is a long way to Orange from where you are but I know you only spent around an hour on the aircraft, I was here, and you are charging my customer $635.00. You must think you are a lawyer or a doctor. By the way even those guys only get paid for jobs they actually finish. I feel I should also mention that I have only used your services on three separate occasions and all three of those customers where not happy with your services or your fees. In fact, I think I may have even lost one of my customers over it, and my relationship with the others has been scarred. XXXXXXX and I decided to split this fraudulent bill of yours since neither of us gained anything from using you and we both lost. I am the one that regretfully, recommended your services, and therefore I am accepting the responsibility of your failure that you are not man enough to do yourself. Furthermore I think I should let you know that I have been in this business for almost forty years and I know a lot of people. I can almost guarantee you, you will not be doing any more work in this area and your business will pay for your arrogance. It is not the money, this amount of money will not hurt anyone worth a grain of salt, it is a matter of principle. Every HONEST business man knows that you will win some and you will lose some. When you make a mistake, it costs you time and money, but as an honest man, you take the loss, swallow your pride, and do what you have to in order to make it right. If you don't do this, not only are you being a thief, but eventually you will not have any more customers. I am considering sending a copy of this letter to every person in my contact list which includes approximately 250 professional aviation business men and women all over the country along with your business information. The fact is, you do not have a case that you could even remotely stand a chance of winning; however XXXXXXX and I feel as though you have already wasted enough of our time and money with your petty nonsense. So you may think you have won but let's find out shall we?

Sincerely,
Dave Boudreaux

    Of course I have no intention of ruining this man's business but this is how I feel when my customers are ripped off. I said all that because I think you should know that no matter how hard you try you will probably not be able to start a business without some opposition. I believe if you let them say what they will and just ignore it, and continue to treat your customers well, that sooner or later they will do themselves more harm than you could do to them yourself. Anyhow, as I was saying, it is very hard to start a business without a lot of support, but that doesn't mean you will have everyone's.

Next, you cannot start a business without money. I am not a gambler, but I will say that starting a business is a gamble because no-one in the world can tell you ahead of time if you will succeed or lose everything you have. No-one makes a lot of money in their business just starting out and therefore you must plan on no, or little income for at least the first year. You will not make enough money to live on the first year especially if you have a family to support. I started my business by pulling all the money from my 401K and I will not tell you that was a wise decision because when you do that you end up paying probably 40% of that to the government in taxes. The reason I did it is because I have wanted to have my own business since I was twenty years old but I was never going to have the funds available to do it. I didn't start my business till I was almost fifty. Maybe that is good because I probably wasn't mature enough, or strong enough before that, who knows. Anyhow, I had to have those funds if I was going to be able to buy the tools and equipment that I needed and also have the money to live on. Still I would not have survived if not for many of those people I mentioned earlier. You would be surprised how fast you can go through $40,000.00 with little or no money coming in. It takes a lot of tooling and equipment to run a FBO. Much of this I purchased new but then I got lucky and found another company that was going out of business and I was able to buy everything they had for $10,000.00. This included probably $50,000.00 worth of equipment that I would not have been able to acquire otherwise. I believe if you treat people well, and try to live a good moral life, that when the time comes God will provide. Still, that doesn't mean everything will go your way. After I had been in business for one year hurricane Ike hit and I lost my house and just about everything else I had. Fortunately, my tools and equipment where in a safe location and I did not lose them. One thing you can count on is you will be faced with many trials and tribulations during this time. All I can say is, you must remain determined and dedicated or you will never succeed.

The next thing is I think you need to have something that makes you different from everyone else trying to do the same thing. The company that I was working for when I decided to start my own business specialized in doing major structural, or sheet metal repairs only. They were a Certified Repair Station authorized to do this sort of work on numerous different types of ACFT but not all. Everyone else in the area that was running Repair Stations or FBO's then either specialized in sheet metal only, or A&P work only. At that time I was the only one in the area, that I know of, that could do both. We did sheet metal, avionics installations, Annual inspections, ACFT restoration, corrosion work, painting, rebuild flight controls, and any and all major and minor repairs and modifications, and ACFT weighing and weight and balance reports. There are not many places you can take your ACFT and have everything done in one place. Anything that we didn't do in our shop, such as interior work, I had several different places that I can take these things to for work and then we could reinstall it in the ACFT at our facility. We also provide Designated Engineering Representative (DER) services for many of our customers. I have worked in places where the owner avoided talking to the customers many times because he didn't have the answers they were looking for. I pride myself in having the answers no matter what the question is, and I will never try to avoid my customers. I was always taught that you should always face your problems head on. You have probably heard someone say, "I started my own business because I didn't want to have a boss and now instead of a boss I have a hundred of them".

That is so true, the customer is the boss and they can be very demanding. I always put my customer's needs first and many times that means working 16 hour days or working 7 days a week in order to meet their needs. If you are going to run a company you must be willing to work anytime and anywhere. That doesn't mean you will always have to, but you must be willing to if that is what it takes to make the customer happy. Keeping my customers satisfied is my number one priority. You must understand if there are no customers, there is no business. I can assure you that some of my employees do not agree and therefore a lot of times I would working long days or weekends when my employees were at home with their families. I don't think the average company runs that way but I also understand that this was my company not theirs and it was my responsibility to make it successful not theirs. I will also say that my employees were dedicated and I didn't mean to make it sound like they don't care because they do, but I will volunteer to work a lot of times so they don't have to. By-the-way, I have a family that wants me home every night too, but luckily, my family understands the dedication required in order for this to work. Sometimes I would be away from home for weeks at a time. Not only do you have to be a certain type of person to do this, but your family must also understand and be willing to make the necessary sacrifices.

Since we are talking about family, my next subject is about dealing with employees, so I may as well begin with hiring family to work for you. Most of the time hiring family doesn't work very well. At one time I had a father and son that worked for me and they fought and bickered all the time. It was all ok with them because that was just part of their relationship. This is not ok on the job because it is very unprofessional. No one is comfortable with conflict and the job site is no place for this type of behavior. Back when my son worked for me, we were together a lot, but he did not argue with me in front of customers, or on the job.

This is not to say that we would always agree about everything, but when we were on the job, I was the boss and he did not dispute that. We may discuss, or even argue about some of these things later on, but not on the job. I will tell you, I am not always the easiest person to deal with and I am not always right, but we did not argue about it on the job. I have had other family members that worked for me from time to time that did not understand this, and let me just say, they don't work for me anymore. Steven is the type to tell other people, including family, "That is not how you should talk to the boss, and if you were working for anyone else you would already be fired." I have heard him tell several people that and he was right. I try to treat the people who work for me as equals. I realize that one of the reasons we owned a business is because we wanted to some day be in a position where we can just be the boss and tell other people what to do. If I have to treat people like I am better than them to get there then I guess I never will. Don't get me wrong, I don't want to be crawling around under airplanes and standing on my head under an instrument panel when I am 70, but I don't feel like I'm any better than anyone else who has ever worked for me and I would never ask them to do something that I couldn't, or wouldn't do myself. Not every job that has to be done is fun. When we were preparing an aircraft for paint there was a lot of nasty work involved like sanding all day long, or using paint stripper. This is part of the job, but when my people are out there doing this I'm out there doing it too. Because of this they respect me more and are much more willing to do the nasty jobs. I think it also helps them because there are many things that we do that some of them may not have done before. They are much more willing and confident jumping in if they are working alongside someone who has done it before and is comfortable with every aspect of the job. (Lead by example)

Like I said about my customers, my employees were my friends and I will help them in any way I can. Many of them, at one time or another, have found themselves in financial distress and came to me for help. I am glad that most of the time I was able to help them. I didn't do it because they worked for me, I did it because they were fellow human beings in need and they were my friends. Many of them still owe me thousands of dollars and I may, or may not ever see some of it. Whether I do or not I feel good about doing the right thing. Money isn't everything. I believe what is important in this life is what you do with what you have and how you treat others. I think someday we will all have to answer to a higher authority concerning what we did with what we had. Even if we don't, part of the reason I do this is because it makes me feel good about me so whether I ever get paid back or not, whether I ever have to answer to anyone or not, I have already received a reward. Does this make me a good business man? No. They say in order to be a good business man you need to take advantage of every opportunity to make or save money no matter who it hurts. If that is true I will never be good at business. I am just thankful that GOD has put me in a position where I have the means to help others on occasion.

    You have seen me mention several times that I considered my company successful. I guess I should explain what I mean by success. I don't mean I am rich by anybody's definition of the word. The fact is, sometimes I wondered how I was going to make payroll. I don't need to be wealthy to be successful. I understand that you have to make enough money to live comfortably. Most people think that money will solve all their problems and if they don't have enough the answer is to make more, not true. The reason most people have money problems is because they spend more than they make. My definition of success is; I made enough money for me and my family to live comfortably (that doesn't mean we can have anything we want, anytime we want, but we can afford what we need). I had enough to be able to help others in need when I saw it. I had enough to pay my employees and invest in my company when the opportunity would arise. I was able to provide a service to my customers at a rate that most other companies won't therefore making flying, and ACFT ownership, more affordable, and more accessible, to more people. I felt good about everything that I did and my customers are all good friends. I love my job and I have a good reputation in the industry. My goal was to eventually build a company that is financially stable enough to allow me to retire comfortably, and allow my son Steven and his family to take it over and live comfortably as well. To me that is success. If this is not success to you then perhaps general aviation is probably not your best option.

The last area I want to cover is being prepared to run your business before you start. It took me fifty years to do this. You need to be confident enough in what you do that you feel you can handle any situation you may run across. To be honest with you, I was never that confident until I worked for companies where I was put in the position where I had no choice but to do it. Many times I had to go out of town and run jobs by myself. The one thing that going to college taught me above anything else is that no one knows everything. However, if you know how to get the information you need to finish the task and enough confidence in yourself to run with it, then you have all you need. The most significant thing I was not prepared for until the last year was I didn't know anything about keeping books, or doing payroll, or paying taxes for a business, or setting up a company. Thank God that first of all, I had a brother and a sister that where running their own businesses so I knew where to go to get educated. My sister, whom I mentioned earlier, Rose Baxter, helped me get set up to run my business on the computer. She and QuickBooks were life savers. I don't know how people found time to do all that is required to run a business without a computer. I am not a computer person, but I have to give credit where it is due. Rose set up all my accounts, showed me how to keep records, do tax forms, do payroll and so on. I kept my own books for several years. I had been trying to find someone to do this for a long time but good help is hard to find. Unless you have run a business before, you have no idea how much paper work is involved. I am glad now, that I had to learn how to do all this myself though, because it took me years to find someone who could do it right, and I could trust. If I had not known what I was doing I would have had no idea if they were doing it correctly or not and would have probably been in a lot of trouble with the IRS and others by now. I'm sure you have heard the horror stories about companies and individuals getting into trouble concerning taxes. Trust me it easy to do. There are payroll taxes, Federal income taxes, Texas Work Force Commission taxes, Social security taxes, sales taxes, property taxes, unemployment taxes, employer taxes, employee taxes, estimated quarterly taxes, and I am sure I haven't mentioned them all. Not only that, but some are paid every week, some every month, some every quarter, and some every year. On top of that, it's not just paying the taxes, but even if you don't owe any taxes you still have to submit the reports which are also due at all different times. All of you people out there who say companies don't pay enough taxes, or their fair share, you have no idea. Forty percent of all the taxes paid in the US are paid by companies. There are some various types of exemptions for hiring employees, or investing money in the company but the companies still pay way more than anyone else. If it were not for some exemptions the smaller companies would not be able to survive at all. I am not saying that you need to know how to do all of this yourself. I am saying that you need to be prepared for it. It is the smaller companies that are the back bone of our nation. If our current president and his cronies continue to try to raise taxes on the businesses and do things like force employers to provide health care and other benefits, we will not survive.

In my opinion, you do not help the economy by extending unemployment benefits and paying people more to stay home than they would make going to work. You do not help the economy by taking money out of the pockets of the people who are putting people to work (companies). You do not help the economy by making the Government bigger and thereby spending money the country doesn't have. You do not help the economy by offering sanctuary to illegal aliens and giving them benefits that American citizens don't get and thereby allowing them to take jobs from legal citizens. I don't think this is being inhumane, we did not invite them here, they came on their own and did it illegally. I believe it is time for America to start putting Americans first. You do not help the economy by refusing to cut the budget and at least try to make a plan to stop spending more than you're making. You do not help the economy by cutting the Military and putting thousands of more people out of work and on the streets. You do not help the economy by robbing Peter to pay Paul by taking more from the successful to give to the unsuccessful. We need to make policies that encourage companies to grow so they can hire workers and encourage the unemployed to get a job so they can provide for their families and have pride again. We do not tell them it is ok if you can't find the job that you want; we will pay you to stay home. My experience has been that there is plenty of work out there for people who want to work and plenty of excuses and opportunities for those who don't. I have had numerous people tell me, "Why should I go to work as long as the government is paying me not to". I'm not saying this because I just think it is true, people are telling me this all the time. True enough, you may not be able to find the job you had when you were laid off, or the dream job you are looking for, or the job that allows you to work at home, or the job that pays what you think you are worth, but you can find a job. I have never been on unemployment in my life and I am no better than anyone else. Unless you are disabled, or have some other impairment, you can find a job, and you can provide for you and yours, and you can be proud again. I think the president is only popular because he tells everybody what they want to hear. It is time for the American people to stand together and face the fact that we can't keep doing what we have been. It is time to take our medicine and do what we have to in order to make America strong and proud again. A good leader is not someone who tries to give everyone what they want. A good leader is a good reader by the way, how can you lead with direction if you have no idea where you are going. The rest of the world now sees America as week, with no direction and lazy. This is not the image I want the world to have of my Country. I want to be proud again.

CHAPTER X
MAKING THE HARD CHOICES

As I said before, I try hard not to burn bridges, but sometimes it is just not possible because you have to stand for what is right and that is not always easy to do. Sometimes what you feel is right is not what the person in charge thinks is right. I want to tell you about an incident that happened my first day on a new job once. Before I get to that I'd like to share with you the interview for that job. I went to an interview for a job at a Certified Repair Station in Oklahoma City Oklahoma at Will Rogers World Airport. I went in and sat down and the person doing the interview was a lady from Human Resources (HR). After the introduction she asked me to sit down and then she asked me, "What do you know how to do?" At that time I had been working on ACFT for about 20 years and had worked on everything from a Cessna 150 to a Boeing 747. I must admit that question caught me a little off guard. I found it rather humorous and had to think a bit before I responded. After a moment, I just looked at her and said, "Do ya'll use maintenance manuals?" She said, "Of course, we don't do anything without the manuals, why you ask?" I said, "I can do anything you have a manual for." She said, "You're hired". I think I have been hired for every job I have ever interviewed for but that had to be the shortest and most interesting of them all.

My first day on this new job, we were working on a McDonald Douglass MD-80. We were all in the cabin installing the seats after a major inspection. The supervisor came up in the ACFT and proceeded to chew everybody out. Let me just say he was not being very nice about it. After he had left I continued to work for a few more minutes and then I decided I wasn't going to work in that type of environment. I stopped what I was doing and told the lead mechanic I was going to go have a word with the supervisor. It was funny because he said, "This is your first day on the job and I guess you want it to be your last too". I told him I don't know about that but I'm not going to be treated that way. I have been in this business too long to deal with that. So I went down and knocked on the supervisor's office door. He looked like he was in a really bad mood, but it was too late, I'm committed now. He told me to come in and then he asked what I wanted. I asked him, "Is this some kind of special occasion, or are you always an ass-hole?" (Pardon my French). He stopped what he was doing and just stared at me for a moment and then he said, "I'm an ass-hole most of the time." Then he started laughing and stuck out his hand for a shake and introduced himself. We became very good friends after that and I worked there for several years. Sometimes you just have to do the right thing. I wish I could say it always turns out that well, but it usually doesn't.

    I had a job with the Civil Service overhauling fuel tanks on the KC-135 which is a Boeing 707 that is modified into a flying fuel tank. They are for refueling other ACFT in flight. It was normal procedure for every new mechanic to start out in fuel tanks and stay there for about the first year then they would rotate out and another new guy would take his place. After working there for three years I was still working fuel tanks and they were starting to make me sick. I was starting to miss a lot of work using my sick time going to the doctor. I was having lots of stomach problems and breathing problems. I had asked numerous times to be removed from fuel tanks but I was told that they would not let me out because I was the only one making sure the work was getting done. It seems like in a lot of places; if you do your job your punished and if you don't they give you a promotion. One day my supervisor came and chewed me out for using all my sick time, which is mine to use, then he proceeded to tell me that my vacation time that I had scheduled six months prior was cancelled. Again, I went back to work but the longer I thought about it the angrier I became. So I went back to his office and I told him I didn't care what he said, I wouldn't be there next week, then I left and went back to work again. I won't mention his name here but I will never forget it. A little while later he came to the airplane where I was working with his boss and started threatening me again about losing my job. By now I'm really pissed. So I came out of the fuel tank and took off my security badge and threw it at him and said, "You want my job take it, cause I'm fixing to sweep the hanger floor with your scrawny little ass". I never thought about it before now, but I guess I like using the word "ass" when I'm irritated. They gave me a week off without pay for being insubordinate and when I got back to work I had to go straight back to the fuel tanks. So this supervisor asked me to come back to his office on my first day back. When I went in he asked me, "Did you learn your lesson?" I said, "I learned how to get time off." Needless to say, I didn't work there much longer. Sometimes you just have to stand up for what is right. I'm not saying I always do it the right way, but it was effective.

 Back when I was in the Air force, it seems like a hundred years ago, I was the night shift supervisor over a squadron of CT39A's. That is a Sabreliner, A Sabre 60 to be exact, anyhow I had an ACFT that was not showing the proper reading on the hydraulic system gauge in the cockpit (that is what we called the part of the cabin where the pilots sit back then but now that is politically incorrect). The gauge in the cockpit is a repeater gauge, in other words, it is a gauge that just repeats the reading in the hell hole. (That is in the tail where the direct pressure gauge is located). They call it that because it is so difficult to work in there. The direct pressure gauge is on the hydraulic accumulator and as the name indicates, it reads the pressure directly off the accumulator. It was my job to make sure that the ACFT which were scheduled to fly the next day were ready to go. One of the maintenance controllers decided that this ACFT was un-airworthy which would have made it impossible for me to meet my schedule. I guess you could say I'm slightly job oriented. I tried to explain to him there was no reason the ACFT couldn't make it's mission but he had to prove he was right. I got aggravated; I know that's hard for you to believe at this point. I told him if he wanted to do my job he could have it and I left. I did not know at the time that he had called the maintenance officer and told him what was going on. As I was leaving the base I was stopped at the gate by the security guards and they held me there until the maintenance officer showed up. The maintenance officer made me go back and we got into the manuals and I tried to show him how the system worked but the maintenance officer was still not sure so they canceled the flight after all. The next day the maintenance officer took the question to the hydraulic specialists and they explained to him how the system worked and that there was no reason the ACFT couldn't fly. About a month later I was called to the maintenance officer's office and he presented me with the Air Force Master Technician Award. What can I say, when you are right, you are right. Because of that incident, a few years later while I was in Germany, I was asked to work on an accident investigation team to determine what happened to a Sabreliner during a routine maintenance run after a phase inspection. The ACFT had jumped the chocks and ran into a crane and burned to the ground, but that is another story.

    That does remind me of another interesting job interview though. While I was there in Germany I was assigned to a squadron that worked on Sabreliners again, as well as C-140's (that is a Lockheed Jet Star). We called them "Junk Stars", anyhow one day I was at the squadron and I was instructed to go to maintenance control and talk to the maintenance officer (here we go). I had no idea what she wanted. So I went up there and when I walked in she said, "I have an opening in maintenance control and I am considering you for the position". I told her I didn't want the job. She said, "Good you're hired". I said again, I don't want the job, She said, "That is why you're hired. If you wanted the job it would mean you are not any good at being a mechanic and you want to do something else. If you don't want the job, it means you like what you do because you are really good at it, and that is what I need. I need someone up here who can relate to what those guys need out there". I told you earlier that I got ever job I ever interviewed for, but you didn't know that I meant even the ones I didn't want. I worked in maintenance control the rest of the time I was in Germany. As it turned out it was actually a good job to have there. It allowed me the opportunity to travel all over Europe and see a lot of things I would have never seen otherwise. The reason is because we worked three on and three off. That work schedule gave me a three day weekend every week and as you probably know Europe isn't very big so you can drive anyplace you want and back in three days.

I could tell you many more stories about standing up for yourself and your employees when you, or they are right, but I think you get my point. One last short story; One place I was working a while back I had a crew of sheet metal mechanics working at a CRS. The Director of Maintenance (DOM) there was a good man but we didn't always see eye to eye. For a long time the DOM along with one of the lead mechanics there picked apart everything my people and I did. I'm not going to say that everything was perfect, it wasn't, and I had no problem fixing, or having my people fix the items that were legitimate. After a while though, it became apparent that they would never be satisfied even if we spent weeks fixing things that were just simply not bad. Every day we would go in to work ready to move forward just to find out that they had found one more little thing they didn't like. At one point I even got an engineer involved to try to explain that the work was acceptable, he said ok, but I still don't like the way it looks and he wanted it done over anyhow. By now my guys were just fed up and didn't even want to come to work. In the meantime, I had several other customers that I had to keep putting off because we could never satisfy this DOM. Sometimes you have to make the hard choices, so I left there with my people. This was a company that I had been doing work far for years and they were one of my best customers. Many of the people there had been my friends for a long time but I had to do what was best for my company at the time. It does me no good to have a job that I can never finish. I cannot make money on a job I have to do over several times out of my pocket just because someone doesn't like the way it looks. When I am doing a sheet metal job for another company, it is because I am the sheet metal specialist. If I didn't know what I was doing I would never be in that position to start with. These people were never in a position where they had to take responsibility for what we did. It was my job and I was signing it off. If it is my signature and my responsibility, then I will have the final say about what is acceptable and what isn't. Unfortunately I am afraid this conflict has burnt bridges, but right is right. Sometimes you have to make hard choices and it will cost you, but you will have to do it anyhow.

CHAPTER XI
CONTRACT LABOR

There are a number of aviation maintenance schools out there that give you, or they used to give you, a fully loaded tool box when you graduated. Instead of a tool box I feel they should give you a motor home. Almost every mechanic out there has had their time on the road. I almost named this chapter "ON THE ROAD AGAIN", but I'm not a huge Willie fan even though I do think he is a good writer. Anyhow, I thought this would be a relevant topic for a number of reasons. To start with, if you are planning on being involved in aviation, whether it is as a mechanic, a pilot, a flight attendant, an engineer, or a business owner, you may as well pack your bags. If you are not one who likes to travel and be away from home a lot, this is not the field for you. This makes it difficult if you are a family man or woman. Many start out in this field when they are single and after they get married they just can't keep doing it. In the industry we see a lot of divorces because of the nature of the business. We call it "AIDS" that is, "Aviation Induced Divorce Syndrome". Seriously, it is no laughing matter and that is why I want to tell you how it will be before you get in. My son Steven worked for me the first year he was married and during that year he probably had not spent more than three days in a row with his new bride at home since the honey moon. Eventually his wife Rachel just gave in and decided to come to work for me also so she could spend more time with Steven. I will get good employees any way I have to (Just kidding). She had started keeping the books for us and since she had been doing that for another business for a long time she became a tremendous help to us. You never know where you will be next week or the week after that. We really loved the travelling as we were able to go to a lot of places, see a lot of things and meet a lot of interesting people. I have to tell you though sometimes you just want to stay home. Personally, I was normally only able to go home one to two days a week. Many times I would not see home for two or three weeks. I had one job that lasted eleven months, that was in Midland Texas where I worked on a restoration project on the only flying B29. They call her "FIFI" and she belongs to the CAF and is based there at the CAF flight museum in Midland Texas. Soon after that I went to an airshow in Houston where I got to see her fly again. It is always nice to see something like that knowing that I had a part in it. We need new dedicated people to get involved in aviation, but we need people who know ahead of time what they are getting into and will stick with it.

 The next thing is when you are a new A&P mechanic it is not usually that easy to find a local job unless you already know a lot of people in the business. The A&P schools will tell you that they have a placement program and they will help find you a job right away. I won't say that they are not being totally honest, but I will say, don't expect that job to be local. I grew up in Houston and there are a lot of aviation companies in this area but they are very well established. It is not likely you will get in unless you know someone. You may see adds in the local paper but I tell you, these companies are looking for people with experience. Sorry, but there is no substitute for experience. After about eighteen years of experience I still had to take a contractor job to get back in the Houston area. I told you I have never been unemployed. What I meant is I was never unemployed other than being between jobs, which was never over a week and I have never been on unemployment. What I didn't tell you is how many different jobs I have had and how many different places I had to go to stay employed. I have been lucky I guess, because all my life any time I left a job there would be two or three companies calling within a day or two with a job offer. Don't expect to be in this business and grow roots anywhere for at least ten years. So starting out, even if you went to school and you have an A&P license you can expect to relocate and usually it will be with a contract agency. Just look on the web under aviation contractor companies and you will see all you care to. The reason for this is because the aviation industry is so tied to the economy and therefore as the economy fluctuates so does aviation. It is also closely tied to the oil industry as many of these companies use corporate jets for their businesses, but even more importantly because ACFT are expensive to operate. Avgas or aviation gasoline is running about $6.00/gal. That may not sound like a lot but when you consider the fact that the average single engine ACFT carries 40 to 80 gallons of fuel. You think it is expensive to fill up your car, that is $240 to $480 for each fill up. The fuel burn is generally around 8 to 16 gals/hr so you figure out how much it cost to go to Grandma's house for the weekend. What I am saying is when the gas prices go up the typical general aviation ACFT owner will stop flying. A lot of companies will also consider different modes of transportation, or sometimes just fly commercial. The other day we had a G4 Gulfstream stop in for fuel; it cost $7000.00 to fill that ACFT with Jet fuel. How many people you know can afford that? When the economy gets bad people quit flying. Because of this a lot of companies will hire contract labor mechanics for a specific amount of time, or for a specific job and when that time or job is over you move to the next one.

 Contractors are also used a lot in the aviation business the same way other businesses use temp agencies and that is to find permanent employees. If you as a company hire a contractor you are under no obligation to provide any benefits or commit to keeping them for any specific amount of time. Therefore you do not have to have a reason to let them go if it doesn't work out. If the company likes the person they can hire them as full time employees and trust me, that changes everything.

Hiring a contractor also eliminates the search for a mechanic. If a company needs a mechanic right away it is easier to just call one of the many contract companies and tell them what you need. That eliminates advertising, interviews, and so, so much paperwork. The contractor will generally make a little more money than the full time mechanic based on a forty hour week. That is because the contractor, if more than a hundred miles from his home will receive perdium (additional living expense pay). A typical example would be $11.00/hr. base pay plus $15.00/hr. for living expenses. That makes your pay $26.00/hr. and that is better than you can do as a new mechanic at any local job. In the long run it is also cheaper for the company because contractors don't get benefits which cost companies a lot of money. The problem with it is you have to be away from home and many times the expenses will be more than what you make. The other thing is you can only collect the perdium for a year. You can keep working there but you lose the perdium. If you want to stay there at the same price you have to leave there for thirty days and then start over. The reason is the Government rules concerning contractors are written that way. As far as they are concerned, if you stay there more than a year it is no longer a temporary job and you have had plenty of time to relocate permanently.

The next thing I want to talk about concerning contract labor is from the business owner's point of view. Obviously, it is much less complicated to hire contractors and much less paperwork required but how do you know if someone is legally an independent contractor or should they be full time employees. Following is a couple of excerpts that I took from the Department of Labor. As you read this maybe it will give you just a little taste of what a pain it is to interpret all the rules and take care of all the paperwork to be an employer. You would not believe all the work that an employer has to do to comply with Government rules, first to hire you, then to keep you own the payroll. Did you know that your employer has to pay more taxes for you than you pay for yourself in some cases? Some tax breaks are for employees, but not for employers.

WHAT'S THE DIFFERENCE BETWEEN AN EMPLOYEE AND INDEPENDENT CONTRACTOR?

An employee is anyone who has agreed to be employed, under a "contract of service", to work for some form of payment. This can include wages, salary, commission and piece rates. Employees are not volunteers, sharemilkers, self-employed or independent contractors, or real estate agents (if their contract says they are an independent contractor).

It is important to be clear about whether you are an employee or an independent contractor, as only employees receive minimum rights and entitlements under employment law.

For more information about determining what is employee or an independent contractor, please see our **Who is an employee page?** page.

WHO IS AN EMPLOYEE

An employee is anyone who has agreed to be employed, under a contract of service, to work for some form of payment. This can include wages, salary, commission and piece rates.

This includes:
- homeworkers
- people who have been offered and have accepted a job
- fixed-term employees
- seasonal employees

- casual and part-time employees
- probationary and trial employees.
- An employee is not:
- a self-employed or independent contractor
- a sharemilker
- a real estate agent whose agreement says they are an independent contractor
- a volunteer who does not receive a reward for working
- in some cases, a person who is engaged in film production.

FIXED TERM EMPLOYEES

If an employer has a genuine reason based on reasonable grounds to offer a fixed term, this should be explained at the start and put in the written agreement. The employment agreement must set out how the employment will end and why.

For example, a job may be for a certain time (e.g. for six months) or until something happens (e.g. when the project ends) or until work is completed (e.g. until the fruit is picked). Such workers have the same rights as other employees, except that their jobs will finish at the end of the fixed-term.

CASUAL AND PART-TIME EMPLOYEES

The rights of full-time employees apply equally to part-time employees. These rights also apply to casual employees, but the way in which annual holidays, sick and bereavement leave are applied can vary for these employees.

It can all be very complicated and confusing. Even with help it is very simple to forget something. If you forget to file a report, even if you don't owe anything, you will have to pay a penalty for not filing the report. Come on, give me a break.

After Hurricane Katrina, two Cajun workers had to relocate to Texas to find employment. They went to work as contractors for a construction company digging ditches.

After a couple of days on the job out in the hot sun they couldn't help noticing that the supervisor was sitting under a shade tree watching them work. So one of them told the other one you should go over there and find out why he is sitting in the shade while we are doing all the work. So the one went over and asked the supervisor the question. The supervisor put his hand against the tree and told the contractor to hit his hand.

The contractor swung but just before the supervisor got hit he moved his hand and the contractor hit the tree. The supervisor said that is why. So the contractor went back to his buddy in the ditch and his buddy said well what did he say? The contractor looked around but there was no tree so he put his hand over his face and said, "Hit my hand".

CHAPTER XII
WORKING FOR AN AIRLINE

As I talk to young people who are interested in being in the Aviation business, it surprises me how they all think the ultimate goal is to be an airline mechanic or pilot. I guess the reason for that is the visibility that the airlines receive through the press. But I can tell you from personal experience that the airline is not for everyone. I think this is the next logical subject to discuss because we just talked about packing your bags. That's right, on the road again.

First, if the airline hires you, you will most likely have to pack your bags to even start. Secondly, even if you have been with an airline for ten years or so, it is still possible that you will still be on the bottom of the seniority ladder. What that means is if the airline decides to cut man power at the station you are at because of the economy or any other reason; you guessed it, pack your bags. If the airline has to lay people off for any reason, at any station, anywhere, pack your bags. The last time I heard on the news, American Airlines just filed for bankruptcy again. If they decide to realign their activities or open a new station, pack your bags. If they get bought out by another airline, or combine with another airline, pack your bags. When I say pack your bags, I mean you will either no longer have a job, or you will have to move to keep your job.

I was with Trans World Airlines for six years and I was still on the bottom. During that time I had to move four times or lose my job. I started in Oklahoma City and then went to St. Louis, then New York, Then back to St. Louis. After that I joined the ranks of the divorced. I can't blame that entirely on working for the airline but it didn't help matters any. Following the divorce it was very difficult for me to stay in the area, so I quit the airline and moved back to Houston.

Another thing about working for the airlines is everything is specialized. I mentioned earlier about how some of the larger maintenance organizations split everything up. The reason for this is they believe that if you have different shops and different mechanics set up it offers the opportunity for each section to become more efficient. This is probably true because if you have all the equipment you need to do a job at your fingertips it takes a lot less time to do the job. If you are a mechanic in this situation and you only have to do one job it is really easy to become proficient at it. From the airlines point of view this is a good thing but I didn't like being an assembly line mechanic. Can you say boring? You have hydraulic specialist, tire shop specialist, sheet metal technicians and so on. I think this limits a mechanic's ability to learn the entire ACFT. This doesn't matter if you have no further ambition. However, if you want to know the entire ACFT, or ever want to become an IA, this type job will never give you the opportunity to get that training or exposure.

Then there is the line mechanic, who is a self-described, glorified gas station attendant. I have known guys that had done this all their lives and that suited them just fine, but I'm here to tell you these folks are not functioning as true ACFT mechanics in my opinion. They are licensed A&P mechanics with all the skills but they are doing work anyone could do. The airline has a thing they call the Minimum Equipment List or MEL. This list tells the mechanics what equipment the ACFT has to have functional in order to fly. When an ACFT comes in during the regular day you have about thirty to forty minutes to fuel the ACFT, do a through flight inspection, check for discrepancies or squawks and get the ACFT back out. I have heard some mechanics refer to this through flight inspection as, "kick the tires and light the fires", and it isn't much more than that. As for the squawks (discrepancies) if this item is not on the MEL list you stick a placard on it and send it on its way. These items will be fixed later when the ACFT returns for the night, or in some cases whenever it goes into a major inspection and is not on the schedule to fly. The line mechanic will do around four or five of these quick turns in a day and the rest of the time he is sitting around waiting for an ACFT to show up. Frankly I got tired of sitting around doing nothing. For some people I guess that is the perfect job but it wasn't for me.

 One other thing I would like to touch on is the fact that as far as I know all the airlines are unionized. That is, everyone belongs to a union. I know everybody has their own opinion about unions and I will probably step on some toes here but I know what I experienced. One of the reasons that airlines have to charge so much for tickets is because everyone that works for the airline has the same benefits and they all make top wages. I don't have a problem with mechanics and pilots (skilled labor) making top money but why bother going through all that training when, if you are a bag thrower with the airline you can make almost the same money and have all the same benefits. Mechanics and pilots spend years training and thousands of dollars getting their liscenses. You can thank the union for that. The mechanics can't get a raise unless the bag throwers can get one. I can't say for sure that all airlines are still that way but they were when I was there.

 In my opinion, the unions today are there to protect the rights of the people who are lazy and don't want to do their job, or are drug users that got caught, or alcoholics who can't leave the bottle at home. The only people I ever saw the union do anything for were those that were in trouble for one reason or another. The airline could not even fire a person who was a known drug addict. If he got caught, even on the job doing drugs, the union would make the airline send them to rehabilitation and keep them on the pay roll. They even had to pay for the rehabilitation. This was true even if they were repeat offenders. I never saw a good mechanic that stayed out of trouble and did his job ever do anything with the union except pay dues. I believe the unions had a purpose in the beginning when there were no rules and the companies did not treat their people well at all. However today they are just turning the American work force into a bunch of lazy bums.

I will give you another example of what I mean. When I worked for the Civil Service on the KC135 aircraft I saw so many things that irritated the heck out of me. Most of it was because of the unions. We had one guy there that worked in the fuel tanks with me. This guy was going to college during the day and working on the fuel tanks at night. I worked with this guy for three years and he was still there when I left. The only two things I ever saw this guy do was either go up inside one of the big fuel tanks and open his college books and study all night long, or sleep. Now you know why they wouldn't let me out of the tanks, someone had to get the work done. So you ask, why I didn't turn him in, well I did. I was told that everybody there already knew what he was doing and they had tried to do something about it but the union wouldn't let them do anything.

On that same job I must have heard a million times, "I'm not doing that, the union says that isn't my job". On Fridays we always had to put all the equipment away and close the hanger up tight because no one would be there until Monday. One Friday I heard on the PA that they needed a fuel man to come to the far end of the hanger for something. This hanger was a mile long and I was on the opposite end. I started walking down there but it took me probably twenty minutes to get there. When I got there I saw six men standing there looking at the door with their hands in their pockets. I asked what the problem was and they said there was an air duct in the door way and they couldn't close the door. I asked why they didn't just move it and they said you guys use those ducts in the fuel tanks, according to the union rules that's not our job. I'm not kidding, I was furious. In my opinion, that is just completely stupid. The Company paid six men to just stand there for twenty to thirty minutes while they waited for me to get there and move the duct. I walked over and kicked the end of the duct out of the door way and walked off. It reminds me of a poster I saw on a bulletin board the other day. It showed a high way with the yellow line on the side of the road that was painted around a stick that was laying there on the shoulder with just a small corner of it on the high way. The caption said, "Not my job". This is what the unions have done to us. A lot of people out there are just lazy screw ups and the union is giving them the tools they need to get away with it. I know a lot of people who love the unions and swear by them because of the benefits and wages they make when they are working and maybe even more important the wages and benefits they make when they don't work. The problem is a lot of the time they aren't working and the companies still have to pay. You still wonder why everything cost so much, I don't.

 Sorry, didn't mean to get off on a tangent. If you don't mind the traveling, or the lack of job security, or the lack of experience you will get, or dealing with the unions and the lazy people, the airline is a good place to work. They do have very good benefits and very good pay scales. To me it's not worth the hassle, there are way too many things more important to me than money.

CHAPTER XIII
EXPERIENCE IS THE KEY

When it comes to finding a job, or getting a job where you want to live, or having enough seniority to stay where you want to experience is the key. With the airlines it is all about seniority but seniority is indicative of experience. When you work at a Certified Repair Station (CRS) or a Fixed Base of Operations (FBO) then the key is how much the company owner values your abilities and again that will largely depend on experience. I think the main reason I don't have any trouble staying employed is not because I'm anyone special, because I'm not. It is because I have a lot of experience and therefore am more valuable to the employers than the average mechanic. Perhaps the other reason is because of the licenses. Not only the Airframe and Power plant licenses, but perhaps even more so the Inspection Authorization. The A&P license and especially the IA certification are also indicative of experience.

By now you must be asking what makes me qualified to write a book on aviation. If I am qualified, it would have to be because of my experience. So let me think about it and I will try to remember what all I have worked on. I went in the Air Force in 1975 and attended basic training in San Antonio Texas and then Tech school in Wichita Falls Texas. After that my first duty assignment was at Peterson Field in Colorado Springs Colorado. It is Peterson Air Force base now. Anyhow, while I was there I started my career working on T-33 trainer airplanes. They were the only ACFT still flying that used a centrifugal flow jet engine. It was a J33A-35 centrifugal compressor engine. Don't ask me why I remember that when half the time I can't remember what I did yesterday. I actually got the opportunity to fly one of these antiques once. It was amazingly responsive. That is the only ACFT I think I ever did a barrel roll in. I was at Peterson Field for three years the first time. I also flew a T-37 while I was there, we called them Tweety Birds because the engines made a loud squealing noise.

After that I went to Alaska and was stationed at a remote site in King Salmon which is a small military base located just above the Aleutian chain. I say remote site because the only way there was by airplane or boat. I was there for about a year and I can tell you that was an experience I will never forget. There was a small Eskimo fishing village there and they actually had a civilian side of the airport. What made it interesting to me was there were 280 men and three women stationed there. Let me just say, three very, very, popular women! While I was there I worked on the F4E Phantom. She was a very impressive ACFT in her day. We called her the lead sled because she was a very heavy ACFT especially when fully loaded with a 30 MM Gatling gun, Four AIM seven Missiles, and Four AIM nine missiles and a center line extended range fuel tank. It was totally awesome, as the kids say these days, when she took off and kicked in the after burners. She would light up the sky and shake the earth. I could really tell you some interesting stories about that place. While I was there I also worked part time for a fishing guide building a lodge, as a bag thrower at the civilian side of the airport and as a waiter at a little restaurant. It got so cold there that you couldn't stay outside for more than two minutes at times. This is also where I saw the biggest snowflakes I ever saw. I could go on and on but that's not my purpose here. If you ever meet someone who served there ask them about the 21 moon salute.

After I left Alaska I went back to Peterson Field. The only reason I was able to do that was because I had a wife that was also in the Air force at the time. She was an ACFT electrician stationed at Peterson Field. Anyhow, when I got back to Peterson I was assigned to a squadron working on the T-39 Sabreliners. For those of you who don't know a

Sabreliner is a small twin engine jet ACFT. I think it carried two pilots and six passengers but don't quote me on that. The engines where J60-P3A's which is a turbojet engine. I will just give you a small jet engine identification lesson here. The Turbojet (TJ) engine is purely a jet engine core only. The Turbofan (TF) is a turbo jet engine core that drives a large fan. The fan actually produces up to 80% of the thrust while the core just turns the fan. This is the type of engine used on practically all commercial and most corporate jets today. They use these because they are considerably more fuel efficient and produce more thrust than the strait turbo jet. A turbo jet is a jet engine consisting of an axial flow compressor that is driven by a turbine wheel. I don't have time to explain all that right now but since all jet engines have the same basic core configuration the terms jet and turbojet are synonymous. The Turboprop (TP) is a jet engine core that drives a propeller. Since the jet engine can turn at speeds of around 30,000 RPM the prop is driven through a reduction gear box. Propellers are generally rotated at 2300 to 3000 RPM. If a prop is turned much faster than that the tips will reach supersonic speeds and the prop loses its proficiency. Don't quote me on these numbers folks because there are all kinds of ACFT designed for all types of conditions and these numbers are for general information not specifics. Anyhow, I was there at Peterson Field for another three years and Most of that time I was the night shift supervisor.

Following that I had my first experience with TWA in Germany. No I don't mean Trans World Airlines. Working for the airline came much later. I mean what we called Teeny Weeny Airlines. If you have never been overseas; all I can say is, if you ever get the chance you should go. I remember walking out of the airport in Frankfurt Germany and thinking holy cow, I feel like Alice in wonderland. The colors were all so unbelievably bright. All the vehicles were fluorescent greens and oranges and so loud. On top of that, the trees and the grass was unbelievably green as well, I had never seen such. Those colors were naturally bright and loud just as the painted colors were. Everything was also very clean. I distinctly recall traveling down the autobahns, through the small towns, down the country roads and thinking there is no trash. There was seriously no trash in Germany anywhere that I saw. In addition the autobahns with no speed limit made life interesting. Ok, back to the point, while I was there in Germany I was assigned to a small squadron that maintained the CT39A's and the C140's. Because of the small size of these passenger jets those guys called themselves Teeny Weeny Airlines or TWA. I worked for TWA about a year and after that I went to maintenance control. While I was there I also took classes through Embry Riddle Aeronautical University to prepare for the A&P tests and worked part time for the local general aviation shop. The mechanic at that shop just also happened to be the FAA Designated Maintenance Examiner (DME) for the area. (Not to be confused with DME, distance measuring equipment). I worked for him for about two years and after I finished the courses and passed the three written exams, he gave me the oral and practical exams. At this shop I worked on small single and twin engine Cessna's and Pipers. If you didn't catch that, there are actually nine tests you must pass to become an A&P mechanic. They are the Airframe, Power plant, and General areas where you are tested by written, oral, and practical exams in each area. The oral and practical exams are usually all given at the same time if you are testing for both licenses at once.

    I was in Germany three years and then I got out of the Air Force and moved to Oklahoma City to go to college. In Oklahoma City I was hired on with the Civil service at Tinker Air Force base. There I worked on the KC135's or Boeing 707's as I have previously mentioned. I worked there for another three years and then I was hired on with the real TWA (Trans World Airlines). I stayed in Oklahoma with TWA for about a year where I worked on Boeing 727's, Douglas Co. DC9's, and McDonald Douglass MD80"s. After that I went to St. Louis Missouri, which used to be where TWA's main hub was located. While I was there in ST. Louis the first time I was a line mechanic doing quick turns on everything from their DC9's to 747"s. Like I said before though, except for a few minor items now and then, a line mechanic doesn't do a lot of work on the airplanes.

I do remember one story I have to tell you though. We had this 747 that came in for a quick turn and they had developed a leak but nobody knew what was leaking. Most of you know a 747 is a two story ACFT in the forward section. Up the stairs is the cock pit (or flight deck), a restroom, and the first class passenger cabin. The people on the lower deck had something leaking from the ceiling on their heads. They obviously didn't know what it was as they were all laughing about it. What it was is blue water which is the chemically treated water that the lavatories are serviced with. If you didn't get that it was toilet water leaking from the upper deck rest room. Like I said, they were all laughing about it so I wasn't about to tell them what it was. We found that a pressure line was broken that was attached to the flush pump on the toilet so we just cleaned up the excess water and placarded the upper deck toilet and sent them on their way. That was what we called, "lickem, stickem and kickem". Again, a million other stories I could tell but we need to move on.

I was only in St. Louis for about a year or so when TWA was forced to down size due to the actions of one Carl Icahn (a corporate raider, but that is another story also) and therefore lay off workers. If I wanted to keep my job I had to move to New York. I lived in a hotel room with four other mechanics for the next year in Long Island New York while working at JFK airport. That life pretty much consisted of going to work in the morning and coming home, taking a shower and hanging out in the hotel bar until bed time. People were afraid to go out at night in that area of town so there really wasn't a lot to do, but I could tell you some good bar stories. Did you hear about the flight attendant that couldn't get out of her hotel room? She said there were only three doors. One was the closet, another was the bathroom and the last one had a do not disturb sign hanging on the knob. Sorry, just a little airline humor. Anyhow, while I was at JFK I worked on Boeing 747's, and 767's and Lockheed L1011's. By-the-way, you may not care, but my favorite commercial aviation ACFT to fly on and to work on was the Lockheed L1011. I think it was the only ACFT built for commercial airlines, at least back then, that was built with the mechanic in mind, although Boeings 767 had some nice features as well. I worked on these ACFT in the hanger while they were going through major inspections and maintenance. This kind of maintenance was much more enjoyable and valuable to me. I just want to also say that I met some great people while I was in New York. They seem to be a little rude and stand-off-ish when you first meet them on the street but I think that is because they don't know who they can trust out there. Once they get to know you they are some of the nicest people you will ever meet anywhere. All these years later I wonder how some of those people were affected by hurricane Sandy.

After that, I went back to St. Louis where I spent the rest of my time with TWA doing major inspections and sheet metal repairs on DC9's and MD80's. From there I worked for several different CRS's and FBO's in the St. Louis and Oklahoma City areas. During this time I worked on many of the ACFT I have already mentioned as well as the Falcon 20 which we did major mods on converting these ACFT from passenger to cargo ACFT. That was in East St. Louis, where we installed cargo rails and modified the fuselage by cutting a large hole in the side of the fuselage and installing a side cargo door. We also built the cargo doors. I was the night shift supervisor there and to be honest with you, until I worked there I had not done a lot of large sheet metal projects. At another one of these CRS's I also did a lot of work on the Bach 111, and the Boeing 737, and the Douglas DC8. In addition I spent a little time in Wichita Kansas where I worked on the Lear 45 while it was still in the test flight stages. It was my first opportunity to work side by side with ACFT engineers.

Eventually, I decided I wanted to come back to the area where I grew up near Houston. Even with all the experience that I had there were no full time jobs available there. The only way I could come back to this area was to take a contractor job. I took a job working on Boeing 707's doing major sheet metal modifications to the wings in Lake Charles Louisiana. That was still about three hours from home but it was as close as I could get. I was there about a year when I got another contract job in Houston working for Continental Express. I hired on there as an A&P mechanic but once they found out I could do sheet-metal that was all I did. There we worked on ATR's and Embraer 120's and 145's. I worked there for a year and I couldn't stay there as a contractor any longer so I hired on as a sheet metal specialist again at a repair station at Hobby airport on the south side of Houston. While I was there I worked on every different type of fixed wing aircraft I can think of. Lets' face it, just too many different kinds of ACFT to mention as well as several different types of helicopters. Maybe I should say just about every type of single and twin engine, reciprocating, and jet ACFT you can think of like: Beechcraft, Cessna, Piper, Hawker, Gulfstream, Lear, Commander, Falcon, Challenger, and Bell. I also worked on a lot of old military ACFT such as the T33, F4E, B29, B17, B24, B25, and so on. This is another place where I had the opportunity to work with a lot of draftsmen and engineers. Working with Aviation engineers is the next topic I want to discuss. I can't remember all the different types of ACFT but if you ask me about a particular ACFT I can probably tell you a whole story about one. Since I left that company and started my own, you can add Piper sierra, Mooney M20, Cirrus SR20, and 22. Bonanza A36, Lancair, Cessna 340 & 421, and Beech Debonair, Aeronca, Decathlon, RV 6 and 8, etc. I have also done, and still do, a lot of transporting ACFT by ferry flight or disassembly and moving them on a trailer. Later I will tell you a few of those stories. I owned my own aviation business in Orange Texas for nearly fifteen years before I decided to sell out and take a job as the Chief of Maintenance in Hood River Oregon for a company called Hood Aero in September of 2022 and that is where I am today.

CHAPTER XIV
AVIATION ENGINEERS

When I started working on ACFT I could have sworn aviation engineers would always be my worst enemies. ACFT, especially the smaller ones can sometimes be extremely difficult to work on. It's actually kind of funny but just about every large shop that you go to will have either a small guy, or a woman that they use to work fuel tanks, or under instrument panels, or other areas that they specialize in. Women are especially handy when you are working in areas where it requires small hands and coordination. Unfortunately there just aren't very many women ACFT mechanics. My company was fortunate enough to find a new mechanic of small stature. Anyhow, my point is the convenience of accessibility does not seem to be a major concern when an engineer designs an ACFT. After working on them for so long a lot of it seems to come natural for me now. I can't tell you how often one of my people has been struggling with a screw or something and I have asked them if they want me to give it a try and most of the time it just falls in. I don't know if it is natural ability, years of experience, or just plain luck. I really don't care either, I just want it done, and most of the time it is easier for me.

An A&P, in most cases will not be working closely with engineers unless he is assigned to a research and development department or perhaps a flight test facility for an ACFT manufacturer as I touched on earlier. A sheet metal technician on the other hand, may have the opportunity to work closely with a Designated Engineering Representative (DER) either directly or indirectly on a regular basis.

Normally it will be the sheet metal supervisor or lead technician that will be contacted by the DOM to perform a metal repair. The lead will then research the item to determine if the ACFT Structural Repair Manual (SRM) has a repair listed that is applicable. If the ACFT doesn't have an SRM then the A&P mechanic's Bible, the FAA Advisory Circular AC 43.13-1b will be checked for an applicable repair. If there are no applicable repairs for the situation in either of these manuals then it will become necessary to have a repair designed. ACFT structural repairs have to be designed and authorized by a DER. Usually, the lead will contact the DER directly and provide whatever information is required to get the repair designed and a drawing to that effect. This information will include the ACFT basic information such as: Type, model, tail number, serial number, etc. In addition, any Structural or Service manual references dealing with the area where the repair will be needed should be included. You will also usually use photos of the affected area and possibly hand drawings, or sketches of the area with particular attention to detail. These drawings must show the length of the crack, (for example) what type of material is affected, the thickness of the material and how close the crack is to the edge of the material. After you have worked with a particular engineer for a while and understand the process, the engineers will also appreciate any suggestions as to what type of repair you have in mind. I have had the pleasure to work closely with a number of engineers now and it is very helpful if both parties understand ahead of time what the process is. Some of the engineers that I have or am still working with are actually quite pleasant. One firm that deals mostly with Turbo-Commanders is G-Tech out of Oklahoma owned and ran by the Gary and Fred Gatz. Another firm that I use often is Georgian Aerospace Group out of Missouri. These folks are a great bunch, give them a shout and ask for Niki, Joel or Bill and tell them Boudreaux sent you. (No seriously that isn't a joke)

 At the very least, if you are a sheet metal man you may not work directly with the engineers but you will deal with their work. When you are in A&P school you will learn a little about reading drawings. At the time you may think you will never use that and you may not depending on what you do in your career. If you do get assigned to work with sheet metal repairs you will be reading these drawings and you will probably find that you didn't get enough training on it. I found this to be the case when I was doing the cargo door mods on the Falcon 20's in East St. Louis. Once I got in a position where I really had to learn it, it wasn't all that hard. Now I don't even have to think about it most of the time. Each engineer will do his drawings a little differently however, so it is best if you can use the same one as often as possible.

I actually worked with one engineer a couple of years ago that still did all of his drawings by hand. Sometimes it was very difficult to read his writing on the drawing or tell what he was trying to depict in the sketches. It has been my experience, and this is how it is usually done these days, that computer aided drafting programs (CAD) are generally the best means to do these drawings. CAD programs are more complicated to use than the average person is going to just jump into and most engineers have their own draftsmen anyhow. I have been in the environment where we did our own drawings but luckily my son Steven is also a computer wiz. He sat down with a CAD program for a couple of hours one night and was able to do complete drawings the next day, but don't expect to be able to do that yourself. I know I can't do it. If you find yourself in the situation where you need to do drawings you can take college classes to learn how. It is truly amazing what you can do with a computer these days (I said you, not me).

The other person who will be working closely with a DER is the IA. The reasons are all the same that I mentioned before because the repairs that require engineering are major repairs. What is a major repair? That is a great question, glad you asked. You see the FAA has its own definition but you had better check with them if you're not sure, or just go ahead and treat it as one anyhow. The Federal Aviation

Regulations (FAR's) do give a definition of what the FAA considers a major repair or alteration but saying it is vague is putting it politely. Never-the-less, they will not hesitate to give you a hard time if you fail to handle this appropriately.

Major alteration. An alteration not listed in the aircraft, aircraft engine, or propeller specifications—
(1) That might appreciably affect weight, balance, structural strength, performance, power plant operation, flight characteristics, or other qualities affecting airworthiness; or
(2) That is not done according to accepted practices or cannot be done by elementary operations.

Major repair. A repair:
(1) That, if improperly done, might appreciably affect weight, balance, structural strength, performance, power plant operation, flight characteristics, or other qualities affecting airworthiness; or
(2) That is not done according to accepted practices or cannot be done by elementary operations.

If it is a major repair, whether you use the ACFT manual, the AC 43.13-1b, or a DER to get approved repair materials, you as an IA must file a FAA Form 337 with the FAA within 48 hours. If you have any doubts as to whether it is a major repair or alteration then you should just go ahead and file one. There is no law against filing one if you don't need it, but if they think you needed it and you didn't do it, you have a serious problem. There are some examples of major repairs listed in the AC43.13-1b but again these examples are susceptible to various interpretation so be careful.

I have included a sample of the FAA form 337 for your reference.

MAJOR REPAIR AND ALTERATION
(Airframe, Powerplant, Propeller, or Appliance)

US Department of Transportation — Federal Aviation Administration

Form Approval OMB No. 2120-0020

For FAA Use Only — Office Identification

INSTRUCTIONS: Print or type all entries. See FAR 43.5, FAR 43 Appendix B, and AC 43.9-1 (or subsequent revision thereof) for instructions and disposition of this form. This report is required by law (49 U.S.C. 1421). Failure to report can result in a civil penalty not to exceed $1,000 for each such violation (Section 901 Federal Aviation Act of 1958).

1. Aircraft
- Make: Cessna
- Model: 182M
- Serial No.: 18259517
- Nationality and Registration Mark: N71165

2. Owner
- Name: Flemming, Ray J.
- Address: 15602 TC Jester Blvd, Houston, TX 77068-1941

3. For FAA Use Only

4. Unit Identification

Unit	Make	Model	Serial No.	Repair	Alteration
AIRFRAME	--- (As described in item 1 above) ---			X	
POWERPLANT					
PROPELLER					
APPLIANCE	Type / Manufacturer				

6. Conformity Statement

A. Agency's Name and Address:
David Boudreaux
12143 Lewis rd
Cleveland, TX 77328

B. Kind of Agency: X U.S. Certificated Mechanic / Foreign Certificated Mechanic / Certificated Repair Station / Manufacturer

C. Certificate No.:

D. I certify that the repair and/or alteration made to the unit(s) identified in item 4 above and described on the reverse or attachments hereto have been made in accordance with the requirements of Part 43 of the U.S. Federal Aviation regulations and that the information furnished herein is true and correct to the best of my knowledge.

Date: 01/4/12
Signature of Authorized Individual:

7. Approval for Return To Service

Pursuant to the authority given persons specified below, the unit identified in item 4 was inspected in the manner prescribed by the Administrator of the Federal Aviation Administration and is ☒ APPROVED / REJECTED

BY:
- FAA Flt Standards Inspector / Manufacturer / X Inspection Authorization
- FAA Designee / Repair Station / Person Approved by Transport Canada Airworthiness Group / Other (Specify)

Date of Approval or Rejection: 01/04/12
Certificate or Designation No.:
Signature of Authorized Individual:

Form 337

NOTICE
Weight and balance or operating limitation changes shall be entered in the appropriate aircraft record. An alteration must be compatible with all previous alterations to assure continued conformity with the applicable airworthiness requirements.

8. Description of Work Accomplished
(If more space is required, attach additional sheets. Identify aircraft nationality and registration mark and date work completed.)

The following structural components of the forward section of the fuselage were removed and replaced with serviceable components: Firewall assembly P/N 0753100-200, L/H and R/H stiffener assemblies P/Ns 0753102-1 & -2, Firewall doubler P/N 0753600-19, Firewall to tunnel L/H & R/H fittings P/Ns 0713632-1 & -2, Upper nose gear reinforcement L/H & R/H P/Ns 0713638-1 & -2, L/H & R/H elevator pulley brackets P/Ns 0713663-1 & -2, L/H and R/H bulkhead assemblies P/Ns 0713603-1 & -2, Nose gear upper fitting P/N 0543013-1, Nose gear lower fitting P/N 0743606-2, Steering boot assembly P/N 0713666-1, L/H lower cowl attachment bracket P/N 0713665-1, Lower forward belly skin P/N 0713334-5, L/H and R/H Tunnel bulkhead assemblies P/Ns 0713631-1 & -2, Lower sprocket L/H bracket assembly P/N 0713677-3, Nose steering bellcrank upper support assembly P/N 0713637-1, Nose steering bellcrank lower bracket P/N 0713636-1, L/H and R/H reinforcements P/Ns 0713290-1 & -2. The following mechanical components were removed and replaced: Nose gear steering bungee P/N 0760622-1, Nose gear fork and barrel assembly P/N SK 182-34, Nose wheel steering dampener P/N 0743024-1. The wings, horizontal and vertical stabilizers, ailerons, flaps, elevators, and rudder were reinstalled. All flight control cables ran and reconnected and all flight controls re-rigged per the aircraft service manual. These repairs did not affect the weight and balance.

-------- END --------

CHAPTER XV
AVIATION SAFETY

I know I have spoken about a lot of things that probably make you think that aviation is scary. I would like to point out that almost all the safety violation issues that I have talked about were involving general aviation ACFT and the general public does not fly on these ACFT. I'm not saying, by any means, that because of that it is ok for people to do these kinds of things. I'm just reassuring you that commercial and corporate aviation is safer. Part of the reason for this is the fact that the airlines not only have the mechanic do the job and an inspector check it behind him, but then a second inspector checks it a third time. They refer to it as RII requirements. I said earlier that some of these airline mechanics, specifically the line guys, were not really functioning as mechanics. I feel I need to make it clear that I'm only referring to the guys that work during the day on the line and their job is to just get these ACFT in and out as efficiently as possible. As I said, they do very little actual maintenance on the airplanes. The actual maintenance is done by the line guys that work through the night after the ACFT are done flying for the day or the guys in the maintenance hangars where major inspections are done. These guys are the real mechanics and the backbone of the airline. The line guys work long hard hours through the night in the freezing cold, or steaming heat, night after night preparing these ACFT to meet the next day's schedule. These guys and gals are extremely thorough, safe and conscientious. I have had to work out on the line when it was so cold that two of us had to take turns doing a job and sitting in the truck with the heater running. We would swap places every ten minutes.

The other thing is the way these ACFT are designed. These machines have backup systems to the backup systems. It reminds me of what Bruce Willis said in the movie Armageddon about NASA. There is a lot of stickem and kickem going on during the day because the way these airplanes are designed and equipped a lot of things can be inoperative without affecting the flight capability or safety of the ACFT whatsoever. It is also true that these ACFT can take a lot of abuse and even damage and still be able to fly. It was obvious during the various wars when ACFT landed safely after being shot full of holes. Some even came back home after having half the tail or half of one wing blown off. I'm not recommending you try that, I'm just saying. ACFT seldom have a catastrophic failure. Most crashes end up being caused by pilot error. It is still by far statistically the safest way to travel. I have spent a lot of time telling you about all the paperwork involved working on ACFT. All of that is for safety purposes. The FAA, the aircraft manufacturers, the maintenance people and the inspectors all work together very closely to identify and correct any problems that ACFT develop before they become a safety issue for the general public. The inspection processes are very thorough, including visual, fluorescent dye penetrant, x-ray, magnetic particle, eddy current, and numerous other advanced techniques.

In addition as I mentioned before, there is a tremendous amount of accountability. Every part that is replaced is carefully tracked and traced through the process of being properly repaired and documented or discarded. Every new part comes with documentation to prove its authenticity. Every part that comes back from repair is tested and checked and inspected and documented by whom the repair was done and the inspector who checked it and the materials used to do the repair. Every repair process has been approved by the FAA or a FAA engineering representative. When deficiencies are identified by the manufacturer they issue service bulletins to each person who owns that type ACFT notifying them of the condition and directions on how to correct them. When mechanics or inspectors identify discrepancies in the field the FAA is notified and the appropriate actions and notifications are processed in an amount of time that is appropriate to the severity of the discrepancy. The FAA issues Airworthiness Directives that require mandatory modifications whenever safety issues are identified on any ACFT that is type certificated. All ACFT maintenance records have to be kept by each ACFT owner for the life of the ACFT. All ACFT repair facilities must keep records on all maintenance performed for a minimum of seven years. This includes maintenance logs for the airframe, the engine/engines, the propeller/propellers, and all accessories. Every person who works on these ACFT or any part of it has to make entries in the ACFT logs including their name and mechanics license number along with the inspector and his number. I can tell you from experience that as far as I know, there is no other maintenance field that takes as much time, or does as much paperwork, or consumes as many resources and effort to insure your safety as aviation does. To be sure sometimes it is a royal pain in the posterior but it is what we do. I may complain about some of what I see some mechanics doing, or what you have to deal with concerning the FAA, but considering what they do to keep the public safe I feel it is all completely necessary. Now you can see why, when an ACFT loses its records, it is only worth half what it was. It is hard to criticize when I can't think of anything else they could do to make it safer. To be sure, people will make mistakes, and machines do break from time to time, but no other machines or mechanics are subject to more scrutiny than in aviation and seldom do things get by. That is why ACFT are still in good shape and flying safely after fifty years of service.

    Many of you probably already know that in some parts of Alaska in the summer time there may be only two hours of darkness and in the winter time only two hours of day light. When I was in King Salmon Alaska during the winter time I got off work one day at seven in the morning and it was still dark. I went back to my living quarters and went to sleep. My clock didn't have any indication of AM or PM on it, it just gave the time. I woke up sometime later and looked at the clock and it said it was seven-thirty. I had no idea how long I had been sleeping but it was still dark. I got up and went out to the game room where a couple of guys were playing pool. I asked one of them, "What time is it?" He told me it was seven-thirty. So I asked him, "Is that AM or PM". He replied AM. Then I asked, "What day is it?" Everyone there got a big laugh out of that. I had only slept for thirty minutes but I truly had no idea.

Boudreaux was out hunting one day and he stumbled across a gold mine and like Jed Clampet struck it rich. So he and his wife decided to have a mansion built and take a European vacation while it was being constructed. So Boudreaux met with the contractor and told him,"Me no concern buot finance much got to have som tings right. At top de turning stairs I got to have de Halo-Statue." The contractor had no idea what he was talking about but didn't want to appear ignorant in front of his customer so he just responded yes sir. So Boudreaux and his wife left and the construction went well all accept the contractor searched everywhere and he could not find anyone who knew what a halo-statue was. After doing a significant amount of research on Cajun history and background he discovered that most Cajuns have had a religious influence in their lives. The fact is most Cajuns are devout Catholics; some of this was probably carried over from their French roots. Anyhow the contractor finally figured it out. So he went to the Catholic Church and asked the priest if he knew where he could buy a religious statue with a halo on it. To make a long story short it took a while but the contractor was persistent and finally found the statue and had it installed. At last everything was ready and the contractor was so proud he could hardly wait for Boudreaux and his wife to come back. So Boudreaux and the contractor met at the house for the grand tour. The contractor showed him the new kitchen with all the latest appliances. He showed him the indoor heated swimming pool, and the fully equipped game room and Boudreaux was very happy but only wanted to see the Halo-statue. As they were heading up the spiral stair case everyone was excited. The contractor was because he had figured out what a Halo-statue was and Boudreaux was because he had always wanted one and never could afford it before. So when they reached the top of the stairs Boudreaux said, "Ma Sha, wat dis is hah? Wer de Halo-statue?" The contractor was disappointed and shocked and said, "I'm sorry sir I thought this was what you meant". Boudreaux said, "No, no, no I mean de tang wat go ringy, ringy, ringy and you put to face an say Halo, Stat U?" (Hello, is that you)

CHAPTER XVI
AIRCRAFT RECOVERY TRIPS

While it is not a lot of fun to be gone away from home all the time, I have been on a number of interesting and enjoyable road trips. One of the first airplanes I went to get was a Cessna 182 in Tennessee. I can't remember the name of the little town but five of us loaded up from the shop in Houston in two different vehicles with trailers and drove straight through to Tennessee. We had a customer who had bought this ACFT after it had hit some trees on approach at that airport. We took the wings and tail off and had the ACFT loaded on the trailers and headed back home in about four hours. You should see the looks you get going down the road with an airplane on a trailer. We had built a sling to load the ACFT with. Once we removed the wings we just attached the sling to the same points that the wings are normally attached to and then we lifted the fuselage with a chain fall from the ceiling joist of the hanger. We loaded the vertical and horizontal stabilizers under the tail on the same trailer as the fuselage and the wings on the other trailer. Anyhow, we had to replace the engine and the propeller and repair the lower cowling that was it. If you are looking to buy an airplane that is probably one of the cheapest ways to get into one. That is to find one that has been damaged in one way or another and hire someone to go get it and put it back together. However, some ACFT are significantly easier to take apart and put back together than others. I would say the average cost of recovering an ACFT is $3000.00 to $5000.00 but again, this can change greatly depending on the distance and type of ACFT.

Some ACFT recoveries are not so cheap or simple, nor can the ACFT be saved. One of my co-workers and I were sent out to recover an ACFT on the beach. I had no idea where on the beach, if it was in the water, or which State it was in, or what kind of ACFT it was. We loaded up and headed out. As it turns out it was a Piper Seneca II that had run out of fuel flying over the Gulf between Lake Charles Louisiana and Beaumont Texas. This is a small twin engine Piper which is a low wing airplane and it had hit the ground while still in about a foot of water and then it came back up and flew another fifty feet or so then crashed into the sand. The landing gear was ripped out from under it but the wings were still attached. Most single engine ACFT are fairly simple to remove the wings from the fuselage because the engine is mounted on the nose of the ACFT. On twins however, another story. Even under ideal conditions removing the wings from a low wing twin means disconnecting two sets of engine controls either in the cockpit and then fishing them all the way out of the fuselage or disconnecting them at the engines and fishing them out of the wings. Neither option is easy or fun especially if half the airplane is buried in the sand.

To make things worse someone had called a chemical spill company to come to the site to remove the ACFT from the scene and do chemical clean up. In my opinion these guys are a joke. First of all, they had brought several large pieces of equipment to lift the ACFT with but they could not get the equipment to the crash site. Second, they had brought a lot of equipment to clean the spill and the ACFT had gone down because it had run out of fuel, there was nothing to clean up. The worst part was they didn't show up until almost dark and they knew absolutely nothing about airplanes. I will say this though, if they were in it for the money they did well. They had about six men and three trucks that were on the clock from about six PM until eight AM and all they did was sit in their trucks and watch us work. I think they told me their bill for that job would be around $15000.00. If I had known that no one was ever going to try to repair this ACFT it would have been much easier to just cut all the connections between the fuselage and the wings. But the reason people call someone like me is to transport the ACFT without causing any further damage. The ACFT was never put back together and I think the main reason is it cost the insurance company so much for the recovery that the ACFT was no longer worth the cost.

When you insure your ACFT you have to place a value on it and that is how much you insure it for. If it will cost more than 80% of the value that you placed on the aircraft to repair it, then the insurance company will usually total it. They will pay you the amount the ACFT was insured for minus what it cost them for the recovery. Then they will send it to a salvage yard to be auctioned off. ACFT are so expensive to repair that more often than not they are totaled rather than repaired. The good thing about that is you can bid on these ACFT and get some good deals but you need to know what you're looking at.

Another recovery that I think was very interesting was a Piper Saratoga that went down in a field in Katy Texas. The ACFT belonged to a doctor and a land surveyor that were partners. I had worked on the ACFT several months earlier when one of the pilots had hit a runway sign. When that happened we had to remove one of the wings in order to do repairs to the wing attach structure and the wing itself. I knew from that experience how much trouble it was to remove the wings on this particular ACFT and therefore I wanted to avoid having to do that again. Anyhow, the engine had failed this time because one of the magnetos (part of the ignition system) had come apart and the pieces went into the accessory drive case causing all the accessories to fail. It is very rare for this kind of thing to happen but now there is an Airworthiness Directive addressing this problem and requiring the magnetos to be inspected regularly and overhauled every five hundred hours.

So this ACFT engine failed and the ACFT was landed in a cow pasture. Other than the wheel pants having some damage and of course the engine, the ACFT wasn't really hurt. There were only two ways to get the ACFT back out of the pasture, either take the wings and tail apart and transfer the ACFT on trailers, or do the work where it was and fly it out. A lot of times an ACFT can be damaged even more when it is disassembled and transported and even if it isn't, it is a lot of work and expense to do the transport. I decided it would be better to do the repairs in the field. So we built a temporary shelter over the ACFT and removed the parts of the gear that was damaged and the engine and propeller. We took the gear parts back to the shop to be repaired and the engine was close to TBO (Time For Basic Overhaul) so it was torn down and shipped to an engine builder. So that took care of the ACFT parts but now how do we get it out of the pasture? I have a brother who, at the time, owned his own company and had the equipment and experience to do landscaping. I hired him to build us a dirt runway, with the land owner's permission of course. After the ACFT was reassembled I had a test pilot fly it out. I would like to mention here, even though I can't remember his name, that this rancher and his wife were very accommodating and understanding people. Good ole southern hospitality. We used his tractor to pull the ACFT out of his field and put it on a dirt road where all the work was done. If you ever read this sir, thank you for your help again. I did go back out there to visit him and his family after I got back in town. Unfortunately I was not able to be there when they actually flew the ACFT out because I had to go to Anchorage Alaska to work on a King Air, but that is another story. I may have to write another book just to tell the other stories.

One other ACFT I had to go take apart out in a cow pasture was a Beechcraft "V" tail Bonanza that went down shortly after takeoff in a cow pasture out in Willis Texas. The ACFT had just had maintenance done to it at a facility in Conroe Texas and the engine failed soon after departure from the Lone star Executive Airport. Anyhow, again I needed my brother's help because it was way off the road and the field was muddy. So we took a back hoe out there and lifted the ACFT in order to remove the wings and then loaded the pieces on trailers. The reason we had to lift it is on a Bonanza the landing gear is built onto the wings not the fuselage. Therefore when you remove the wings there is no way to support the fuselage. The ACFT is relatively easy to disassemble, (other than a few things like the aileron servos for the auto pilot) but it does require special tooling to remove the wing attach bolts. The majority of the damage to this ACFT was the landing gear as cow pastures aren't exactly the smoothest runways. There was a lot of damage to the nose gear and it's retracting mechanisms and linkage, and some damage to the nose bowl. Other than that the ACFT didn't have that much damage considering where it had landed. This ACFT was repaired and reassembled and is still flying today as far as I know.

Talking about not letting anyone who doesn't know what they're doing recover your airplane reminds me of another story. I had a customer that was flying a Cessna 177 Cardinal into Hooks airport in Tomball Texas when his engine quit. He was already on approach when it happened but couldn't make the airport. The only place he could find to put the airplane down was on a busy street in town. So he lined the airplane up with a street where the cars were all stopped at a red light. He was trying to go over the light but was losing altitude too fast to make it so he had to aim for going under the light. Just before getting to the light a truck pulled out in front of him pulling a trailer with lawn equipment on it. So he went under the light in between the highline poles and then pulled it back up and went over the truck and trailer. As soon as he got past the truck he lost all of his airspeed and the airplane stalled and he hit the ground pretty hard but he was able to maintain control. He stood on the brakes but there was another vehicle in front of him and when the man in the vehicle saw him he hit the brakes. Now there was no place to go and no way to stop in time, so to avoid oncoming traffic he veered to the right and his right wing struck a telephone pole and spun the airplane around causing the nose wheel to hit the curb.

He called me quite shaken up and asked me what he should do. I told him whatever you do don't let anyone move the airplane and I will be there as soon as I can. So I rounded up a couple of guys and a couple of trailers and headed that way. When I got there I found that the right hand wing was crushed from about four feet in to the wing tip, and the nose gear was broken off. The windshield was about half way popped out of the frame and there were wrinkles in the fuselage. The cops were all over the place and they had been taking pictures of the airplane with a cop car behind it with the lights on pretending they had pulled him over for a traffic stop. The FAA was also already there and doing their investigation to determine what caused the accident. Thank God everyone was ok and he had done what I told him and not allowed anyone to touch the airplane. The cops had wanted to hook a wrecker to the airplane to get it out of the road but the pilot wouldn't let them. When I got there the guys I brought with me and I turned the airplane around and pushed it up over the curb into the grass to clear the road and then we started to disassemble the airplane. We took the wings off but had no way to lift the airplane onto the trailer. So we just put the nose on the trailer and tied it down so it could turn going down the road but couldn't slide off the trailer. It was about 15 miles down city streets and highways to the airport that the pilot had been headed for which was where the airplane was based. We hauled it all the way to the airport with the nose on the trailer and the main gear still on the ground like we were pulling a trailer. Now that was an interesting trip and talk about some strange looks. We went past several cops and I was sure we would get pulled over but they just looked at us funny like "what the heck" and kept going. As it turns out the airplane was totaled anyhow but we got it back home within three hours from the time of the crash and without causing any more damage.

One of my customers bought an airplane that had been totally disassembled for paint and restoration but the project had been abandoned. That happens a lot since there are a lot of people out there who get into projects like that without having any idea how much work it is and how expensive it is. It was a Piper PA28-180 that was located in Georgia about 20 miles from the coast and just north of the boarder of Florida. Anyhow, we went to pick the plane up and the guy had the whole airplane sitting on a boat trailer, wings, fuselage, tail and all. There was not one part of that airplane that was not taken apart. Most of the parts were there but everything had to be redone. It took us two years to finish going through everything and put this airplane back together and paint it. But I'm telling you this is one of the nicest little airplanes I have ever flown in and it sure is a pretty little thing. About a year later this same customer and I went to California and picked up a 182 which we also disassembled and hauled back on a trailer. It had run off the runway and the nose gear collapsed and destroyed the firewall and the forward belly skin. There was also quite a bit of structural damage in the nose. You can see pictures of this aircraft on the trailer if you go to our web site at www.boudreauxaviation.com.

Just like the rest of the stories I have told you I could go on and on but I want to talk a little bit about ACFT that we have had to get off runways because of gear up landings or other accidents. They range everywhere from a tire blowing out to gear up landings. Many times there are incidents on the runways and taxiways where the ACFT really isn't damaged that bad. However because they were in a hurry to clear the runway they got someone out there to move the ACFT and ended up destroying it. Remember the movie airplane when they were going to push the ACFT off the runway with dozers and the mechanic was furious. That really hit home with me, it does happen a lot. Several years ago I had one airport where there were two airplane incidents in two days. One was a Cessna 188 tail dragger. These ACFT are often used for spraying whether it is for crops or mosquitos. Anyhow, tail draggers have a reputation for ground loops and other ground incursions. In any case, the pilot was on his takeoff roll and for some reason he lost control and hit a runway sign. The sign ripped off the left hand main landing gear and tore up parts of the fuselage and the left horizontal stabilizer, not to mention damage to numerous other smaller items. My guys had to come out in the middle of the night and get the airplane off the runway and back to the hanger. My company ended up doing all the repairs on that ACFT and I have had the opportunity to do a lot of other work on that ACFT since then.

    Back to the point, the next day another airplane that belonged to one of my customers had an incident. The pilot was an instructor and was giving a flight lesson to my customer. The ACFT was a Beechcraft Sierra which is a single engine low wing airplane with a constant speed propeller and retractable landing gear. To make a long story short, the instructor was flying the ACFT and just plain forgot to put the gear down. The ACFT bellied in and it tore up all kinds of things. Again we were called out and this time we used a crane to lift the ACFT and then lowered the gear manually and towed it back to the hanger. I had just finished doing an annual inspection on that airplane and a lot of other major work on the wing attach points due to an AD. We also did all the work to repair this ACFT and both of them have been flying for about a year now with no problems. I know it sounds strange that a pilot would just forget to put the gear down but you would be surprised how often that happens. Fortunately this type of incident seldom ever results in any injuries but it causes a significant amount of damage to the aircraft. As a sheet metal man I have probably had to fix more ACFT because of gear up landings than just about any other thing. There have been a number of those who ran out of gas but seriously there are very few who had serious damage because of a mechanical failure. One more story and then I'll move on.

 A few years ago I got a call from a guy I used to work with and he had recommended me for a job out in Brookshire Texas at the Houston Executive Airport. This pilot had just bought a Mooney M20J. This is another single engine low wing ACFT. The guy had hit a runway sign on approach to the airport. I'm not even sure how you can do that, but on top of that he didn't even know he had done it. He had done a full stop landing and was taxing back out to take off again. There was a student pilot doing training that same day and got in line behind him to taxi to the runway when he saw fuel pouring out of the Mooney's wing. He called the guy in the Mooney on the radio and told him about his situation and the Mooney turned around and taxied back in. His right hand wing inboard skin had two very large holes torn into it and one of them was right through the fuel tank. This particular ACFT has wet wings, meaning that part of the wing structure itself is the fuel tank. Just for your information, the Mooney is American made and at that time was still the fastest single reciprocating engine ACFT in production. Anyhow, we also got that job and ended up re-skinning a large portion of the right hand wing. It seems like in this business your work and word of mouth is the best advertisement. We have done several other jobs at that airport since then. Which reminds me; Not long after that I saw on the news that another airplane had an accident out there and may need some work. This one may be tied up with the FAA for a while though. My understanding is it ran off the runway and the nose gear collapsed and tore up the engines and the propellers and some structure on the nose. But the interesting part is the pilot bailed out and ran off leaving the ACFT just sitting there. When the FAA showed up they found about two hundred pounds of marijuana on the airplane. They may not even ever find out who the airplane belongs to. Funny how that brings me to my next topic and that is drugs and airplanes.

CHAPTER XVII
AIRPLANES AND DRUGS DON'T MIX

I know smoking dope is the cool, and hip thing to do these days. Well, I will tell you if you do drugs don't even consider a career in aviation of any sort. Almost all aviation businesses have a drug testing program in place. The FAA regulations require a testing program for all maintenance personnel who work on any ACFT that fly passengers commercially. Under these programs you will be required to pass a drug test before being hired. I guess many of the men and women that live in Washington and Colorado will be looking for new jobs. I remember a few years back I had a young friend who was trying to find a job so I tried to help out. I am always willing to help those who are trying to take care of themselves if I can. I took her to a place to fill out an application and she came out with a stack of paperwork to fill out. She told me that she basically got the job but she didn't want it. I asked her, "Why did you go to the interview if you didn't want the job". She said, "I didn't know I would have to take a drug test and I smoke pot so I know it would be a waste of time". I told her she should not be doing drugs and I will never forget what she said. "Smoking pot isn't really doing drugs everybody smokes pot". I made it perfectly clear that not everybody smokes pot and I took her home and that was the end of that. So what is wrong with smoking pot? First, it impairs your judgment, second it is addicting, and third it is illegal at least in most places. So then you say, but I'm not doing it at work, and I say pot stays in your system for weeks at a time.

Now you say, I don't think it is any worse than alcohol and I say people who can't handle there alcohol shouldn't drink either. The main difference is you can drink alcohol the night before and the next day at work there is no trace of it in your system. If you smoke pot, the next day it is in your system and if you have to go take a drug test you will fail. In the aviation business failing a drug test is a big deal. In most places it simply means you don't work there anymore. In the rest of the places it means you will be taken off any safety sensitive jobs and will not be allowed to touch an airplane again until you finish a drug rehabilitation program. Then you will be constantly monitored and tested for drugs regularly. When I owned my business, if anyone worked for me and they got busted for drugs or failed a drug test, they were fired, period!

The other times you will be tested on the job are randomly, or after an accident, or if for any reason your actions on the job causes a person in authority to be suspicious that you may be impaired for one reason or another. The random testing is basically a consortium of people in the industry that are all thrown into a big pot and every week a few people are picked from the pot to be tested. If your name is picked you must immediately stop what you are doing and go report to the testing facility for the test. There have been times I had to go be tested three consecutive weeks straight and other times when I have not gone for months. By-the-way, I have never had to worry about passing a drug test and in my opinion if you are concerned about that then you don't belong in aviation. It's not just because I think doing drugs is a bad thing but also because I think my career is more important than any drugs. Some small aviation maintenance companies don't really need their own drug programs because if they work on passenger carrying ACFT for another company they have to be tested under their programs. They would not be allowed to work on that type ACFT unless it is for a larger company through a contract. I have had a drug program in the past however and even though the regulations only required my people to be tested when they were selected, I requested for at least one of my people be tested once a month. Do I believe in drug testing? What do you think? As

I said, the other two occasions for testing are if your actions make you suspicious, or if there is an accident. That is pretty much self-explanatory but I can guarantee if you get in an accident at work and especially if there are injuries or damage to property you will be tested for drugs. If you fail you will be fired and be held liable for all medical and repair expenses.

   Just because I said drugs are worse than alcohol it doesn't mean alcohol is ok either. It is never ok to drink on the job. I know one drink won't make you drunk, but for some people one drink can alter their judgment and slow their reflexes. More significant than that though is the fact that there will be customers showing up from time to time (hopefully) and drinking on the job is very unprofessional. I have known a number of people who went out and had drinks for lunch every day. I didn't think it was ok then and I still don't. I consider that drinking on the job because it doesn't get out of your system before you get back from lunch and other people can smell it on your breath. Some people out there, as soon as they see a drink in your hand or smell it on your breath, they will think you must be an alcoholic. If you can't go through a work day without having a drink then they may be right.

   I say drinking is wrong for those who can't handle it. The problem is no one puts themselves in that category. Even if they don't sometimes their actions do. I think this is important enough to talk about a little more. I have known so many people that are really good people when they aren't drinking, but because of their drinking they have caused many problems for themselves and those they care about. Many families destroyed, many lives lost, many reputations marred, many jobs lost, many accidents caused because of good people who can't control their drinking. I am no expert folks, but I have been trained in identifying drug and alcohol users and abusers. More importantly than that I have lived with them and worked with them over and over again. If you don't know if you have a problem with alcohol or not, check this out:

1. Can you just drink one or two and stop without craving more?
2. Do you have more days a week that you drink than you don't?
3. Do you often wake up in strange places and don't remember how you got there?
4. Do you get in fights every time you drink even with your best friends?
5. Do you usually start with just a beer and end up going to hard liquor almost every time?
6. Do you have hobbies or other activities you enjoy that doesn't involve alcohol?
7. Do you have to drink to have a good time?
8. Do you drink and drive?
9. Do you drink when you're alone?
10. Do you only go to parties where people are drinking?

If you recognize that on occasion, you have been guilty of one or two of these but not regularly then you are probably not at risk. If this describes your everyday life and has been for as long as you can remember, I think you may have a problem. I believe there is more than one kind of alcoholic. There is the alcoholic that can't have fun unless he is drinking and therefore drinks almost every day. Then there is the alcoholic that really doesn't drink that often but every time they do they do something really stupid. I don't think there is anything wrong with drinking for those who can handle it and just do it on social occasions. For those who can't drink responsibly it is just as bad as any other drug. In any case, aviation is no place for people who are addicted to alcohol or drugs. We deal with things that could cause someone to die every day. Even if you don't get caught by a drug test, or a DWI, or some other way, you are putting peoples' lives at risk. That is why the FAA has all of these rules and that goes for mechanics as well as pilots. Ask any pilot you know what the "eight hours bottle to throttle rule is". **DRUGS** and **AIRCRAFT** just **PLANE** don't mix. (That was a play on words.) Even if you take a drug legitimately for an illness you had better have a prescription for its use. I have good friends offering me things to help me sleep or get over headaches or other things all the time. I always ask if it is a prescription drug. If it is then there is no way I'm taking the chance. Even if I wasn't concerned about drug testing I believe in practicing what I preach. I will not use prescription or illegal drugs of any kind unless I'm dying and then only if the doctor says to. Personally I think that is a good rule.

CHAPTER XVIII
THE CUSTOMER IS ALWAYS RIGHT

I believe if you are going to be successful in any business your customer should be the most important thing. In the aviation business you do not become successful by getting new customers all the time. You become successful by having customers who keep coming back. When I was a kid in school I would get in trouble occasionally (I know that's hard to believe) and when I got home I would be in trouble again. I know it doesn't work that way anymore. Anyhow, I would try to explain to my Dad that it wasn't my fault and the teacher was wrong and I will never forget what he would say. "The teacher is always right, even when they're wrong they're right". Then I would be punished again. I'm not saying that you should let a customer talk you into doing something that is illegal or unsafe, but you should always be willing to do anything that is safe and legal to their airplane that they want.

When I owned my business, I would often have customers who wanted to upgrade their avionics and what they wanted to do would cost more than what their airplane was worth. The thing about it is you will seldom ever get as much back on avionics when you sell an airplane as what they cost you to install. I think a good avionics package makes the ACFT more sellable even in a bad economy but it doesn't increase the overall value of the ACFT all that much. The same could be said about new interiors and paint jobs. One of the reasons I believe this, is the fact that you can't anticipate what type of avionics the next owner prefers and each pilot has his own preferences. The other reason is avionics and electronics are constantly being upgraded so even if you get the top of the line equipment this year, a year later when you decide to sell your aircraft all of the new equipment you bought is now outdated. You can try to explain that to the customer just so he knows what the future holds and he will appreciate the input but the fact of the matter is he wants it anyhow. If that is the case then just support him all the way and go for it whether you agree with the decision or not.

Even now, as Chief Maintenance for Hood Aero, I go through great lengths for my customers to keep them satisfied. You would not believe the hours I spend during my own time researching different products so I can advise them of what their best options are. As I said, aviation is constantly changing, not only in avionics, but also in regulations, policies, accessories and so on. As advanced as aircraft are these days we need to understand that aviation has only been around for about 100 years. I think in many ways our society is still learning to deal with all the different aspects of it. It is difficult and time consuming sometimes to stay up to date with everything. At any time I could be looking into the options for mounting a portable radio charging dock in a 182 for one customer and the cost of an STC (Supplemental Type Certificate) to install a leading edge landing lite for another customer and the process required for starting an engine on a SOAP (Spectrometric Oil Analysis Program) on a Cessna 182 for another. This is a typical week for us. In my spare time I am also doing AD research on an ACFT engine that has no log book history (What a pain). Oh well, as one of my old bosses use to say, "I see no financial reason why you can't be in seven places at one time".

Not only am I the resource that my customers come to for advice on their ACFT and the options they have, but I am also Johnny on the spot. They know that they can call me any time twenty-four hours a day seven days a week and I will be there for them for information, suggestions or emergency services. I had one customer who was a new pilot and had his own Cessna 182. He was well aware of my policy and took full advantage of it. Every time he went out of town on a trip in his airplane he called me two or three times with questions about his airplane. He would be the first one to admit that he knows nothing about airplane maintenance and he depends on me for everything. I don't mind this at all because it makes me fairly confident that I have a customer for life. Some of his concerns are trivial but some are legitimate too. He contacted me once concerning excessive oil consumption so we looked into it and even though all of his compressions were normal when we rotated the engine for the checks with the lower plugs removed one of the cylinders puked oil all over the place. We ended up having to pull the cylinder and found all the piston rings were lined up. This happens with horizontally opposed engines more often than most think but it really isn't that big of a problem if you catch it and fix it right away.

Back then it was also advantageous that we had our own airplane and could usually be available to any of our customers anywhere within an hour or two. On one occasion we finished an annual on a Piper 140 that had a lot of other work done as well. The ACFT had been sitting for over two years since it had been damaged by hurricane Ike. Two of my customers had decided to buy this airplane as a project but didn't know much about the airplane and have little experience flying one of that type. Anyhow, when we finished the ACFT neither of them wanted to fly it home so we put a pilot in their airplane and a pilot in ours and we basically did a test flight on the Piper at the same time we took it home for them. We used the second ACFT as a chase plane, first for a safety measure in case anything went wrong with the Piper and second in order to have a way back home ourselves. Our customers were elated over the whole thing. The good thing about that is both of these guys also had their own ACFT besides the Piper. One is a Cessna 210 and the other is Cessna 206, from that time on I started taking care of both of those ACFT as well. I can't even begin to tell you all of the times we have jumped in the airplane and went to one airport or another to go take care of some minor thing that had a customer stranded. It seemed like a small thing to us but when they are stranded somewhere it is a big thing to them. Customer loyalty and satisfaction, in my opinion, is what builds a company.

 If you ever get a chance to run a company you will become overwhelmingly familiar with the phrase, "You win some and you lose some". What that means is sometimes you will make money on a job and inevitably sometimes you will lose. Unfortunately, to some degree you have to trust that people will pay their bills but that isn't always the case. I had a lot of money on the books that I will probably never see. Some of these jobs where finished over twelve years ago and still no money. I couldn't even tell you how many times I have heard people say 'oh well you can just write it off.' People think that businesses never really take a loss on anything because they can use it as a tax write-off, not true. When you do a job for a customer and the customer refuses to pay that loss is not tax deductible. If you run your business on a cash basis for accounting purposes, which is what most small businesses do. The only thing you can write off is the money you spent on the job to do it out of your pocket. A write off doesn't mean you can deduct that amount from your tax bill. What it means is the money you spend to do business is not counted as taxable income. So if you spend $1000.00 to do a job out of your pocket and you never get paid for the job, then at the end of the year you can deduct $1000.00 from your taxable income. If you made fifty thousand dollars in the year you will pay approximately 30% of that in taxes at the end of the year which is $15,000.00. If you deduct the $1000.00 you spent then your taxable income is $49,000.00 and 30% of that is $14,700.00. That means if you spent one thousand dollars out of your pocket to do the job and at the end of the year you can, "write off", as they say $300.00. No matter how you look at it that is a net loss of $700.00 to me.

Wait, that's not all. Let's take that same job and say I was planning to charge $5000.00 for the job, one thousand for the expenses, two thousand for the labor which I have to pay my guys to do the job and I hoped to make two thousand in profit. I now spent three thousand dollars on this job one thousand in cash and two thousand in labor. Since I never received the two thousand in profit I can't count it as income and so therefore I can't write it off as a loss. In other words as far as the IRS is concerned it never existed. So now I have lost one thousand dollars in parts and an additional two thousand dollars in labor I never got paid for. Since I spent that money on the business, that income is no longer tax deductible so it saves me $900.00 in taxes at the end of the year. To sum it all up it costs me $5000.00 to save $900.00 dollars in taxes. That is a net loss of $4100.00 which is not a write-off. This is how every business I know of operates but I'm not a CPA and I know accrual accounting is different so you may want to have your CPA check it anyhow.

Now back to the point, there are a lot of times that I will do jobs for some of my customers that I will not make any money on at all. I will give you another example. I have a customer that owns a Piper PA28-180 that we now take care of. The first time I met him he saw us on the airport taking care of someone else's airplane so he stopped and asked me if I knew anyone that could work on small engines. I told you I was a jack of all trades and so I told him, "yea me". He had a little gas powered tow tug that he used for pulling his Piper in and out of his hanger but it had broken down. He was an older gentleman and it is impossible for him to move his airplane without his tug. So I told him I would take a look and it took me the better part of a day to find out what was wrong with it and chase down parts and fix it. At my shop rate that is way more than anyone wants to pay to get a tug fixed. So I charged him $75.00 and sent him on his way. We had never worked on his airplane before but since then he became one of my most frequent customers. The way I see it sometimes you have to be willing to lose a little, not only for the sake of those at your mercy, but also for the opportunity to open other doors. Not to mention, on an airport things get around rather quickly and a good reputation is essential to success. By the way, that is also not a write off.

Boudreaux and Thibadeaux were neighbors and Boudreaux had a horse for sale. He sold it to Thibadeaux for $400.00. Thibadeaux fed the horse oats and fattened him up and the horse was looking really good so Boudreaux bought him back for $500.00. Boudreaux gave him a trim and combed him out and he looked so good Thibadeaux decided to buy him back for $600.00. A few weeks later Boudreaux asked Thibadeaux about the horse and Thibadeaux told him that he sold it to Fontenot. Boudreaux said, "Why you did dat we was both making a good livin off dat horse. I guess Boudreaux had to write it off.

CHAPTER XIX
EMPLOYEE PROBLEMS

Again this will be a topic that will apply to practically any business, but aviation because of the FAA regulations, has its own set of unique challenges. How do you catch a strange colored rabbit? Unique up on it. I know that was bad, but I have to break up the monotony somehow. In today's society, with so many people out there with little or no work ethic at all. It is hard to find employees that are just honest and won't lie about their time on the job, or steal from you. As a working supervisor, owner, boss, whatever you want to call it and frankly I don't have time to babysit or monitor what everyone is doing all the time. I must therefore have people I can trust on the job. I think the fact that most people these days who work in your office will spend at least half of their time on the job playing on the computer, or shopping online, or anything else they can find to do other than their job is dishonest and despicable. As for as I am concerned these people are stealing from you. The sad part is you can't find anyone who knows how to do the job that won't do that to you. I have actually known some secretaries who spent the whole day shopping online for themselves using a company credit card. In my opinion that person should be in jail along with any other common thief. I had one secretary/book-keeper that I had doing inventory because she needed the money, (she was just a contractor not a fulltime employee) but I tried to help her out and I didn't have any book work for her to do. Anyhow, I hired her to do inventory on some stock that I had. This was just busy work for her not something I needed done at the time. In the mean time I had to go work on another job out of town. Each day she would show up at the warehouse around ten o'clock, go to lunch around noon, come back around two, and leave at four. I had other people there that were telling me when she came and when she left. I didn't really care how much time she worked so I didn't say anything to her about it. At the end of the week she turned in forty hours of labor time. So I called her up and I told her I had documented the times that she had worked and she was going to have to pay me back for the money that she had received and not earned. If she would do that I would forget the incident or she would have to find another job. When I got back in town I found out that she had taken probably a thousand dollars worth of items home in supposedly inventory and bring back. Well, needless to say, I never heard from her again. I do my best to help out the people who work for me and for the most part, I have gained their respect and I respect them, but I can't tolerate this sort of thing.

    I have had other employees that I have given them the opportunity to do jobs out of town with the understanding that there will be living expenses associated with that. I offered to pay them travel expenses to the job site and gave them a place to stay while they were there. In some cases I have had employees who went out of town (about a hundred miles from home) with the understanding they were going to stay in the place I provided for the week. Come to find out, when I got there times at the end of the week they had charged me for travel time every day for the entire week. I ended up spending more in travel time than I made on the job. On top of that they were only on the job for about four hours because they had to spend the other four on the road every day. When I asked one of them about it he replied; "I can't stay away from home, my wife likes me home every night". Well guess what, mine does too, but I can't survive if a job cost more to do than what I make on it and most customers don't want to pay for that much travel time every week. In each case I paid them what I owed them and took the loss, but I could no longer send them on jobs out of town. Come on folks, I am just an average guy trying to survive just like you are. I will help anyone in any way I can but don't take advantage me, please.

The next problem is finding people who are qualified to do the work. You already know that you have to have a license to work on most ACFT unless you are under constant supervision. Like I said before, I don't have time to babysit everyone all the time but I can't send just anyone out on a job by themselves. Unfortunately sometimes the mechanics may be just as capable, or even more capable than I am on some things, but it doesn't matter, the regulations are clear. I understand the reason for the rules and I'm not saying they are bad rules. I'm just saying that even if you have someone you can trust, even if that person is well qualified to do the job if he or she doesn't have the license they still can't do it without you there. That means I can't hire any more people than I am able to watch continuously, or I have to hire licensed mechanics only. The goal of every company is to expand. In aviation, you cannot expand unless you hire licensed mechanics and there are at least two small problems with that. First, good A&P mechanics or licensed structural mechanics are very expensive for the average small business to acquire. Even though they don't make as much as most other licensed mechanics it is still a large expense for a small business. That is why most mechanics work for larger companies that take care of either commercial ACFT or corporate ACFT. To be straight forward about it that is where the real money is as far as aviation is concerned. Plus most of these larger companies can afford to offer benefits where the smaller business owner can't. On top of that you have the fact that aviation is very specialized. Therefore even if you find an experienced licensed mechanic it doesn't mean he will be trained in the areas that you need him for. So you hire him anyhow because your company can't grow unless you do. Now you are paying higher wages to a licensed mechanic but you still can't send him or her out on a job by their self because they have not been trained to do the task that you have for them. A license doesn't mean you know how to do everything. In addition there are still lots of things that an A&P is not allowed to do without supervision. One of the things that small shops do to bring in a steady income is annual inspections. A&P mechanics cannot do annual inspections. Again, nothing wrong with the rules, I understand the necessity of them but it still makes it difficult for a small aviation business to grow.

The other problem is licensed A&P mechanics and sheet metal mechanics are getting very hard to find. There are a lot of good mechanics out there but not enough. Unfortunately there are quite a few that are licensed but they only have a limited amount of exposure, that is their training is often concentrated in one or two areas. Therefore you cannot send these guys out on a job alone and expect them to be able to handle any scenario. One of the reasons I decided to write this book is to encourage more potential candidates to become aviation technicians. There is a tremendous shortage in the field and I want to encourage anyone who has aviation in their blood to continue to pursue it as a career. We seriously need more mechanics and pilots, at the same time I feel if you know ahead of time what to expect, it should encourage those of you who fit the profile. It may also discourage those who are just exploring the possibility but had no idea what you were getting into. If you can read all of this and still have the bug I think there is a good chance you are what we are looking for. If this material has caused you to lose interest then aviation is better off without you and like wise. I sincerely hope that the majority of those who read this will have the desire to pursue it more than ever, if so we are more than willing to do whatever it takes to help you get there.

There was this Texas rancher who was having a business meeting with his personal banker and CPA at his house. He was discussing the possibility of expanding his operations and possibly making some investments in some other businesses in the local area. In the middle of their conversation he stopped what he was doing and got up and walked to the window and yelled out "green side up" then came back and sat down. This meeting was quite in depth and taking a significant amount of time and yet every ten minutes or so the rancher would stop everyone and get up and go yell out the window "green side up". After a while the Banker was starting to get a little irritated because the meeting was taking so long due to the constant interruptions. Finally the banker couldn't take it anymore so the next time the rancher stopped the conversation and got up and yelled out the window "green side up", the banker asked him, "What is that all about, why are you yelling out the window green side up". The rancher said, "Oh it's nothing I just have a couple of Cajuns out there that I hired to plant grass".

CHAPTER XX
WHAT CAN I DO ON MY OWN PLANE

What a wonderful age we live in with all the technology and information at our fingertips. Everything you want to know about aircraft and the regulations pertaining to them is all available on line. The problem is you can't find any of it unless you know what to look for. In this chapter I am going to show you everything the Federal Aviation Regulations say that you, as an FAA certified pilot, (not a student or recreational pilot) can legally do to your own aircraft. Before I do that however I want to recommend some reading on line that was put out by the FAA called "Plane Sense". Following is a list of the topics covered in this document. I think most of you as aviation enthusiast will find some information that will interest you. You can find this document on line simply under "Plane Sense":

PREFACE...III
ACKNOWLEDGMENTS...V
INTRODUCTION VII
CHAPTER 1:
AIRCRAFT OWNER RESPONSIBILITIES............. 1-1
    Documentation... 1-1
    Aircraft Registration... 1-1
    14 CFR.. 1-2
    Logbooks... 1-2
    Aircraft Insurance... 1-2
    Reporting Aircraft Accidents/Incidents............... 1-2
    Accident.. 1-2
    Incident... 1-2
    Contacting the NTSB.. 1-2
    Filing NTSB Form 6120.1................................... 1-3
    Aviation Safety Reporting System.......... 1-3

Purpose.. 1-3
Confidentiality....................................... 1-3
Filing an Incident Report...................... 1-3
Safety... 1-4
Safety Hotline.. 1-4
Safety Information................................ 1-4
Reporting Stolen Aircraft/Equipment..... 1-4
Law Enforcement.................................. 1-4
Insurance Company............................... 1-4
Aviation Crime Prevention Institute........ 1-4
Aircraft Registration Branch.................. 1-4

CHAPTER 2:
BUYING AN AIRCRAFT............................2-1
Selecting the Aircraft............................. 2-1
Where To Look.......................................2-1
Factors Affecting Resale Value.............. 2-2
Overhauls... 2-2
Aircraft Records.....................................2-2
Aircraft Title.. 2-2
Filing Ownership and Lien Documents... 2-3
When a Lien Is Recorded........................2-3
Releasing a Recorded Lien..................... 2-3
Aircraft Documents................................ 2-3
Bill of Sale or Conditional Sales Contract.... 2-3
Airworthiness Certificate........................2-3
Maintenance Records............................. 2-3
Manuals..2-4
Airworthiness...2-4
Maintenance...2-4
Pre-Purchase Inspection.........................2-4
Light-Sport Aircraft............................... 2-4
Amateur-Built Aircraft...........................2-4
Military Surplus Aircraft........................2-5

CHAPTER 3:
AIRWORTHINESS CERTIFICATE........................ 3-1
    Classifications of Airworthiness Certificates..... 3-1
    Standard Airworthiness Certificate............... 3-1
    Special Airworthiness Certificate................... 3-2
    Issuance of an Airworthiness Certificate........... 3-3
    Applying for an Airworthiness Certificate....... 3-3
    FAA Form 8100-2,
    Standard Airworthiness Certificate............... 3-3
    FAA Form 8130-7,
    Special Airworthiness Certificate................... 3-3
    Regulations and Policies............................... 3-3
    Title 14 of the Code of Federal Regulations..... 3-3
    FAA Orders (as revised).............................. 3-3
    FAA Advisory Circulars (ACs) (as revised).... 3-3
CHAPTER 4:
AIRCRAFT REGISTRATION............................. 4-1
    Aircraft Registration Branch....................... 4-1
    Eligible Registrants.................................... 4-2
    Registering Your Aircraft 4-2
    Registration Number.................................. 4-2
    How To Form an N-Number........................ 4-2
    Other Requirements 4-2
    Special Registration Number....................... 4-2
    Requesting a Special Registration Number..... 4-3
    Placing the Special Registration Number
        on Your Aircraft.............................. 4-3
    Aircraft Previously Registered
        in the United States...................... 4-3
    Chain of Ownership................................... 4-3
    Replacement Certificate of Aircraft Registration 4-3
    Aircraft Previously Registered in
        a Foreign Country........................ 4-3
    AC Form 8050-1, Aircraft
        Registration Application............. 4-4

AC Form 8050-3, Certificate of Aircraft Registration..................	4-4
Amateur-Built Aircraft Registration and Inspection...............	4-4

PLANE SENSE

Light-Sport Aircraft Registration......................	4-5
State Registration Requirements.....................	4-5
Additional Information...	4-5

CHAPTER 5:
SPECIAL FLIGHT PERMITS........................... 5-1
    Circumstances Warranting a Special
        Flight Permit................................. 5-1
    Foreign-Registered Civil Aircraft.................. 5-2
    Obtaining a Special Flight Authorization........... 5-2
    Application for Airworthiness Certificate.......... 5-2

CHAPTER 6:
LIGHT-SPORT AIRCRAFT................................ 6-1
    Definition.. 6-1
    LSA Certification................................... 6-1
    LSA Registration................................... 6-1
    Available Resources................................ 6-2
    Light Sport Aviation Branch, AFS-610......... 6-2
    Experimental Aircraft Association............... 6-2
    Regulatory Guidance............................... 6-2

CHAPTER 7:
AIRCRAFT MAINTENANCE............................ 7-1
    Maintenance Responsibilities...................... 7-1
    14 CFR Part 91, Subpart E......................... 7-1
    Manufacturer Maintenance Manuals............ 7-2
    Preventive Maintenance............................. 7-2
    Inspections... 7-2
    Annual Inspection................................... 7-2
    100-Hour Inspection................................ 7-2

Condition Inspection..	7-2
Other Inspection Programs..................................	7-2
Progressive Inspections.......................................	7-3
Altimeter System Inspection...............................	7-3
Transponder Inspection.......................................	7-3
Preflight Inspection...	7-3
Repairs and Alterations.......................................	7-3
Minimum Equipment List/.	
Configuration Deviation List.............................	7-3
FAA Resources...	7-3
Experimental Aircraft..	7-3

CHAPTER 8:
MAINTENANCE RECORDS................................. 8-1

Responsibilities of the Aircraft Owner...............	8-1
Logbooks...	8-2
Airworthiness Directives.....................................	8-2
Safety Directives..	8-2
Service Bulletins..	8-2
FAA Form 337,	
Major Repair and Alteration..............................	8-2
Entries into Aircraft Maintenance Records........	8-2
14 CFR Part 43, Section 43.9, Content, form, and disposition of maintenance, preventive maintenance, rebuilding, and alteration records (except inspections performed in accordance with part 91, part 125, §135.411(a)(1), and §135.419 of this chapter...	8-3
14 CFR Part 43, Section 43.11, Content, form, and disposition of records for inspections conducted under parts 91 and 125 and §§135.411(a)(1) and 135.419 of this chapter..	8-3
14 CFR Part 91, Section 91.409, Inspections..	8-3

14 CFR Part 91, Section 91.411,
    Altimeter system and altitude reporting
    equipment tests and inspections................... 8-3
14 CFR Part 91, Section 91.413,
    ATC transponder tests and inspections......... 8-3
14 CFR Part 91, Section 91.207,
    Emergency locator transmitters..................... 8-3
Amateur-Built Aircraft.. 8-4
Available Resources.. 8-4

CHAPTER 9:
AIRWORTHINESS DIRECTIVES.......................... 9-1
    Types of ADs Issued... 9-1
    Standard AD Process.. 9-1
    Emergency AD... 9-1
    Superseded AD.. 9-2
    Compliance with ADs... 9-2
    Amateur-Built Aircraft....................................... 9-2
    Summary of ADs... 9-2
    Obtaining ADs... 9-2

CHAPTER 10:
SERVICE DIFFICULTY PROGRAM...................... 10-1
    Background.. 10-1
    FAA Form 8010-4,
    Malfunction or Defect Report............................ 10-1
    Maintenance Alerts... 10-2
    Background.. 10-2
    Accessing Maintenance Alerts........................... 10-2
    Contact Information.. 10-2

CHAPTER 11:
OBTAINING FAA PUBLICATIONS
AND RECORDS.. 11-1
    Advisory Circulars.. 11-1
    Airworthiness Directives.................................... 11-1
    Temporary Flight Restrictions........................... 11-2
    Notice to Airmen.. 11-2

14 CFR	11-2
Handbooks and Manuals	11-2
Aircraft Records	11-2
Request Aircraft Records	11-2
Format	11-2
Airman Records	11-3
APPENDIX A:	
FAA CONTACT INFORMATION	A-1
APPENDIX B:	
REGULATORY GUIDANCE INDEX	B-1

Now for what all you aircraft owners and operators have been waiting for. This is a list of the preventative maintenance items that the FAA says you can do with your aircraft. I have been hesitant to share this information with some folks because many people out there think they have the ability to do anything. Let me caution you, even though I encourage you to know as much about your aircraft as possible, (which is why I also encourage owner assisted annuals), **DO NOT ATTEMPT TO DO MAINTENANCE YOU'RE NOT FAMILIAR WITH.** You may think that anyone can change a tire because you do it on your car all the time. Changing a tire on an aircraft is nowhere near the same. An aircraft does not have lug nuts and the axle nut must be torqued properly. An aircraft doesn't have a spare and the wheel must be split apart to change the tire. If the tire, tube and wheel are not properly aligned during assembly you will have an uncontrollable shimmy during takeoffs and landings. If the wheel halves are not properly assembled and torqued they can blow apart during inflation and cause serious injury and destroy the wheel. This is just one example but if you have not done some of these things before then I suggest you have a qualified mechanic do it with you the first time, or as many times as it takes for you to feel comfortable with it. All of this information can be found in the CFRS under 14 CFR Part 43 Appendix A Subpart C. Good luck.

INTRODUCTION

According to 14 CFR Part 43, Maintenance, Preventive Maintenance, Rebuilding, and Alteration, the holder of a pilot certificate issued under 14 CFR Part 61 may perform specified preventive maintenance on any aircraft owned or operated by that pilot, as long as the aircraft is not used under 14 CFR Part 121, 127, 129, or 135. This pamphlet provides information on authorized preventive maintenance.

HOW TO BEGIN

Here are several important points to understand before you attempt to perform your own preventive maintenance:

First, you need to understand that authorized preventive maintenance cannot involve complex assembly operations.

Second, you should carefully review 14 CFR Part 43, Appendix A, Subpart C (Preventive Maintenance), which provides a list of the authorized preventive maintenance work that an owner pilot may perform.

Third, you should conduct a self-analysis as to whether you have the ability to perform the work satisfactorily and safely.

Fourth, if you do any of the preventive maintenance authorized in 14 CFR Part 43, you will need to make an entry in the appropriate logbook or record system in order to document the work done. The entry must include the following information:

- A **description** of the work performed, or references to data that are acceptable to the Administrator.
- The **date** of completion.
- The **signature, certificate number, and kind of certificate** held by the person performing the work. Note that the

signature constitutes approval for return to service only for work performed.

Examples of Preventive Maintenance Items

The following is a partial list of what a certificated pilot who meets the conditions in 14 CFR Part 43 can do:
- Remove, install, and repair landing gear tires.
- Service landing gear wheel bearings (for example, cleaning and greasing).
- Service landing gear shock struts (for example, adding oil, air, or both).
- Replace defective safety wire or cotter keys.
- Lubricate items not requiring disassembly other than removal of nonstructural items (for example, cover plates, cowling, and fairings).
- Replenish hydraulic fluid in the hydraulic reservoir.
- Apply preservative or protective material to components where no disassembly of any primary structure or operating system is involved, and where such coating is not prohibited or contrary to good practices.
- Replace safety belts.
- Replace bulbs, reflectors, and lenses of position and landing lights.
- Replace or clean spark plugs and set spark plug gap clearance.

Maintenance Aspects of Owning Your Own Aircraft
- Replace any hose connection, except hydraulic connections.
- Replace and service batteries.
- Make simple fabric patches not requiring rib stitching or the removal of structural parts or control surfaces.

(Note: For balloons, this includes making small fabric repairs to envelopes as defined in, and in accordance with, the balloon manufacturer's instructions and which do not require load tape repair or replacement.)

- Replace any cowling not requiring removal of the propeller or disconnection of flight controls.

Sample Checklists

Propeller Check

Check the following items:
- Spinner and back plate for cracks or looseness.
- Blades for nicks or cracks.
- Hub for grease or oil leaks.
- Bolts for security and safety wire.

Engine Check

Perform the following tasks:
- Preflight engine.
- Run up engine to warm-up and check the following:
- Magnetos for RPM drop and ground-out.
- Mixture and throttle controls for operation and ease of movement.
- Propeller control for operation and ease of movement.
- Engine idle for proper RPM.
- Carburetor heat or alternate air.
- Alternator output under load (for example, landing light in "on" position).
- Vacuum system (if installed) for output.
- Temperatures (CHT, oil, and so on) within proper operating range.
- Engine and electric fuel pumps for fuel flow or fuel pressure.
- Fuel selector, in all positions, for free and proper operation.
- Remove engine cowling. Clean and check for cracks, loose fasteners, or damage.
- Check engine oil for quantity and condition. Change oil and oil filter; check screens.
- Check oil temperature "sensing" unit for leaks, security, and broken wires.

- Check oil lines and fittings for condition, leaks, security, and evidence of chafing.
- Check oil cooler for condition (damage, dirt, and air blockage), security, leaks, and winterization plate (if applicable).
- Clean engine.

Maintenance Aspects of Owning Your Own Aircraft
- Remove, clean, and check spark plugs for wear. Regap and reinstall plugs, moving "top to bottom" and "bottom to top" of cylinders. Be sure to gap and torque plugs to the manufacturer's specifications.
- Check magnetos for security, cracks, and broken wires or insulation.
- Check ignition harness for chafing, cracked insulation, and cleanliness.
- Check cylinders for loose or missing nuts and screws, cracks around cylinder hold-down studs, and broken cooling fins.
- Check rocker box covers for evidence of oil leaks and loose nuts or screws.
- Remove air filter and tap gently to remove dirt particles.
- Replace air filter.
- Check all air inlet ducts for condition (no air leaks, holes, and so on).
- Check intake seals for leaks (fuel stains) and check clamps for security.
- Check condition of priming lines and fittings for leaks (fuel stains) and check clamps for security.
- Check condition of exhaust stacks, connections, clamps, gaskets, muffler, and heat box for cracks, security, condition, and leaks.
- Check condition of fuel lines for leaks (fuel stains) and security.
- Drain at least one pint of fuel from each fuel filter, each fuel tank sump, and any other aircraft fuel drain into a

clean, transparent container to check for water, dirt, wrong type of fuel, and any other type of contamination.
- Visually check vacuum pump and lines for missing nuts, cracked pump flanges, and security.
- Check crankcase breather tubes and clamps for obstructions and security.
- Check crankcase for cracks, leaks, and missing nuts.
- Check engine mounts for cracks or loose mountings.
- Check engine baffles for cracks, security, and foreign objects.
- Check wiring for security, looseness, broken wires, and condition of insulation.
- Check firewall and firewall seals.
- Check generator (or alternator) and starter for security and safety of nuts and bolts.
- Check brake fluid for level and proper type.
- Lubricate engine controls: propeller, mixture, and throttle.
- Check alternate air source "door" or carburetor heat to ensure that the door has a good seal when closed.
- Check door operation.
- Reinstall engine cowling.

Cabin Check
Check the following items:
- Cabin door, latch, and hinges for operation and worn door seals.
- Upholstery for tears.
- Seats, seat belts, and adjustment hardware.
- Trim operation for function and ease of movement.
- Rudder pedals and toe brakes for operation and security.
- Parking brake.

Maintenance Aspects of Owning Your Own Aircraft
- Control wheels, column, pulleys, and cables for security, operation, and ease of movement.
- Lights for operation.
- Heater and defroster controls for operation and ducts for condition and security.

- Air vents for general condition and operation.
- Windshield, doors, and side windows for cracks, leaks, and crazing.
- Instruments and lines for proper operation and security.

Fuselage and Empennage Check
Check the following items:
- Baggage door, latch, and hinges for security and operation; baggage door seal for wear.
- Battery for water, corrosion, and security of cables.
- Antenna mounts and electric wiring for security and corrosion.
- Hydraulic system for leaks, security, and fluid level.
- ELT for security, switch position, and battery condition and age.
- Rotating beacon for security and operation.
- Stabilizer and control surfaces, hinges, linkages, trim tabs, cables, and balance weights for condition, cracks, frayed cables, loose rivets, and so on.
- Control hinges for appropriate lubrication.
- Static ports for obstructions.

Wing Checks
Check the following items:
- Wing tips for cracks, loose rivets, and security.
- Position lights for operation.
- Aileron and flap hinges and actuators for cleanliness and lubrication.
- Aileron balance weights for cracks and security.
- Fuel tanks, caps and vents, and placards for quantity and type of fuel.
- Pitot or pitot-static port(s) for security and obstruction.

Landing Gear Check
Check the following items:
- Strut extension.
- Scissors and nose gear shimmy damper for leaks and loose or missing bolts.

- Wheels and tires for cracks, cuts, wear, and pressure.
- Hydraulic lines for leaks and security.
- Gear structure for cracks, loose or missing bolts, and security.
- Retracting mechanism and gear door for loose or missing bolts and for abnormal wear.
- Brakes for wear, security, and hydraulic leaks.

Maintenance Aspects of Owning Your Own Aircraft
Functional Check Flight

Check the following items:
- Brakes for proper operation during taxi.
- Engine and propeller for power, smoothness, and so on during runup.
- Engine instruments for proper reading.
- Power output (on takeoff run).
- Flight instruments.
- Gear retraction and extension for proper operation and warning system.
- Electrical system (lights, alternator output).
- Flap operation.
- Trim functions.
- Avionics equipment for proper operation (including a VOR or VOT check for all VOR receivers).
- Operation of heater, defroster, ventilation, and air conditioner.

General

Perform the following tasks:
- Ensure that the aircraft is in compliance with all application Airworthiness Directives (ADs) and that compliance has been properly documented in the aircraft records. If the AD involves recurring action, know when the next action is required.
- Comply with recommended service bulletins and service letters. *(Note: These are recommendations unless an AD requires compliance.)*

- Ensure that a current FAA-approved Flight Manual or Pilot's Operating Handbook with all required changes is aboard and that all required placards are properly installed.
- Check that the Certificate of Airworthiness and Aircraft Registration are displayed. Check for an FCC radio station license, if required for international operations.
- Verify that all FAA-required tests involving the transponder, VOR, and static system have been performed and entered in the appropriate aircraft records

Summary

It pays to take good care of your engine. Good maintenance is not cheap, but poor performance can be disastrously expensive.

If you are unqualified or unable to do a particular authorized job, you must depend on competent and certificated aircraft maintenance technicians to perform the job. Always use FAA-approved parts.

You can save money and have a better understanding of your aircraft if you participate in the maintenance process.

Maintenance Aspects of Owning Your Own Aircraft

If you do some of your own preventive maintenance, do it properly. Make sure that you complete the job you start and that you make all the required record entries.

Money, time, and effort spent on maintenance pay off and ensure that your aircraft will have a higher resale value if you decide to sell.

Remember, a well-maintained aircraft is a safe aircraft. A safe aircraft needs to be flown by a competent and proficient pilot. Maintain both your aircraft and yourself in top-notch condition.

Additional Reading
- Advisory Circular (AC) AC 20-106, *Aircraft Inspection for the General Aviation Aircraft Owner.* (http://www.airweb.faa.gov/Regulatory_and_Guidance_Library%5CrgAdvisoryCircular.nsf/0/33172CD8A28FD290 862569BD00687151?OpenDocument).
- 14 CFR Part 39, *Airworthiness Directives.*
- 14 CFR Part 43, *Maintenance, Preventive Maintenance, Rebuilding, and Alteration.*

Once there were these two Cajun carpenters putting siding on a house. One was the supervisor and the other was a hired laborer. The laborer would pull one nail from his pouch and nail it in and then the next nail he would pull it out of the pouch, look at it for a second and then throw it away. The supervisor caught him doing this and asked him what he was doing. The laborer told him that those nails that he was throwing away had the heads on the wrong end of them. The supervisor said you idiot, don't you know those nails go on the other side of the house. Good help is hard to find.

CHAPTER XXI
WHY DO I LIKE GENERAL AVIATON

I told you previously that the best money is in Commercial and Corporate Aviation, so why do I like General Aviation best? One reason is because of the customer base. Like I said before, these guys are not just my customers they are my friends and here is why. This customer base of men and women are just normal people like me and my son who love their machines. They are not millionaires that don't really care about the machines and just view them as another means of transportation or money making tools. They have made great sacrifices to own and operate their ACFT and they love them like they are part of the family. If you know any ACFT owners or private pilots then you know what I mean. It takes a tremendous amount of dedication and commitment to own an ACFT for your own personal use. Not only because of the cost to keep the ACFT in good mechanical condition but also the expenses involved in operating one. Fuel and keeping your ACFT avionics up to date all adds up. There is also the commitment of staying current with pilot regulations and training. We have concentrated on the regulations and restrictions on the maintenance side of aviation. Let me just say all the rules that apply to mechanics also apply to pilots and ACFT owners.

These guys count on me to keep them advised and safe, in other words, they put their lives in my hands. I said earlier that I would not just jump in anyone's ACFT and go fly but I think I should say here that I will be glad and even excited to get to fly in any of my customers' airplanes at any time. Just like I said about not asking any of my mechanics to do anything that I wouldn't do, I would never expect my customers to fly in an airplane that I wouldn't be willing to fly in. There are times when I will send an ACFT off to fly without me because I don't have a choice. One of those times is when an ACFT requires a functional check flight, or a test flight. The FAA does not allow passengers to go on these trips. That doesn't change the fact that if I didn't feel the ACFT was ready and safe to make this trip it would not have my blessing to fly. Another time is if the ACFT is flying on a ferry permit and again the FAA rules do not allow passengers on these trips. One last time is if the ACFT paperwork is not done. I have often been doing paperwork and in the process have found that certain tasks had not been completed. That is why we use checklists for everything. The FAA is very strict about paperwork being complete and up to date before the ACFT flies. That doesn't make the ACFT any safer but it forces accountability. The main reason I won't do this is because I value my license and as we have already discussed the FAA doesn't play around when it comes to rules.

If these customers put as much value on their airplanes as I do then we all look at maintenance the same way. I told you some stories earlier about mechanics and owners doing substandard work, or arguing about what items had to be fixed before an ACFT can fly. I don't know if you noticed or not but none of these guys were my regular general aviation customers. If I explain to my owners something needs to be repaired they say you do whatever you need to. Most of the time these guys are even more concerned about the condition of their ACFT than I am. These are the kinds of customers that are consistently calling me to ask if I can fix this little thing or that rather than trying to hide it from me. I personally don't like having to convince an owner that something is not safe and why I think it needs to be fixed. With these owners I am the go to guy and they trust me. Most of the corporate aviation guys that I have dealt with treat you like they think you are trying to steal their money by making them do maintenance they don't need.

Call me crazy, but I'd rather not have their money than for them to think I'm trying to rip them off.

    I had one guy that had a blow out on the runway at a small airport and the airport manager called me to come take care of it. My son Steven and I took off from the job we were on and drove to our airplane about forty miles away. We got in our airplane and flew to another airport to get a tire and tube to fit his airplane which was about another thirty miles away. We then flew to the airport were his airplane was located around 120 miles away. We gathered up all the tools and went out and jacked the ACFT and replaced the tire and tube on the site. Then we moved the ACFT back to his hanger and flew back to our home base and drove back home. Taking off the job that Steven and I were on costs the company around $400.00. The tire and tube we bought for the plane cost around $300.00. The cost to fly the ACFT to three different airports was around $120.00. I felt it was not practical to charge this guy all that to fix a flat, so I charged him the cost of the tire and tube and for two hours of labor which came out to around $450.00. This guy went all around the airport telling folks how I took advantage of him and ripped him off. This is not, and never will be, one of my customers. Oh yeah, he is a corporate business owner. His pilot has asked us to do work on his ACFT a couple of times since then, not gonna happen. To put it in simple terms, I want to work for people who trust me and appreciate me. Back when I owned my business I would tell people this; No I'm not rich, but God has put me in a position where I can choose my customers. For so many years I had to do work for people that were rich jerks because my boss wanted their money. Well, not anymore, I don't have to, and I won't work for jerks. OK, that may be more why I have my own business than why I like general aviation best, but I wouldn't want my own business if I didn't have these choices. I'm not sure why, but I have found that a lot of large company owners and people who have lots of money are just a pain in the #$%^&%$#@ and I won't deal with it. Some things are more important than money to me. My co-workers and I are some of the best there is at what we do and we are honest. If you can't treat us with respect don't call, we don't need you, I don't care how much money you have.

The last reason and I won't go into too much detail about this, but because of the FAA regulations General Aviation is less stressful. As many rules as we have to deal with in General Aviation, in the Commercial and Corporate sectors it is worse. One example I will give you is the fact that I can work on General Aviation ACFT with my A&P license and I can do major repairs, alterations, and annual inspections with my IA. This is all you need in General Aviation to run a FBO. With Corporate and Commercial Aviation it is much more complicated. For our purpose here that is all you need to know. From a beginner's perspective, you will not be dealing with all that and I want to encourage you to come join us and learn to love and enjoy aviation the way my customers, my co-workers and I do. I hope you have learned just enough about the aviation industry to be able to decide whether it sounds like it is for you or not. I really don't think you will have to think about it much. Either you have the bug or you don't. If this didn't spark your interest at all See Ya, and if it did, See Ya Round.

Boudreaux and Trosclair were a couple of drinking buddies who worked as aircraft mechanics at de Bayou Teche, Louisiana, International Airport. One day the airport was fogged in and they were stuck in the hangar with nothing to do. Boudreaux say, 'Man, I wish we had something to drink!'

Trosclair say, 'Me too. Y'know, I've heard you can drink de jet fuel and get a buzz.'

So dey pour demselves a couple of glasses of high octane gas and get completely smashed.

De next morning Boudreaux wake himsef' up and is surprise at how good he feel.

In fact he feel GREAT! NO hangover! NO bad side effects. Nuttin!

Then de phone ring. It's Trosclair. Trosclair say, 'Hey, how you are this morning?'

Boudreaux say, 'Man, I feel great, how bout you?'

Trosclair say, 'I feel great, too. You don' have a hangover?'

Boudreaux say, 'No dat jis' fine Is great stuff — no hangover, nuttin'. We ought to do dis more often..'

Trosclair say, ' Yeah, well dey's just one t'in g.'

'What's that?'

'Have you farted yet?'

'No.'

'Well, DON'T – 'cause I'm in Shreveport!'

CHAPTER XXII
FLYING A TWIN

During the last few years of running my business I had the distinct privilege of coming to know a kind elderly gentleman named Thomas J. Almond, commonly known to his friends simply as Tommy. Tommy was in his late seventies when I met him. He had owned a farm near Orange Texas before I knew him and he had served as a crew chief on a bomber B-47 as I recall so he and I had a lot in common. I first met Tommy because after he sold his farm one of the last things that he had wanted to do his whole life was to own an aircraft and Tommy had fulfilled his dream by using some of his farm money to purchase one of his all-time favorite aircraft a Cessna 337 Sky Master. Tommy had been mechanically inclined his whole life, but he had never gotten his A & P license and so he came to me to have some work done on his Sky Master. After that he and I became best friends in no time at all. Tommy even came to work for me for a short time before he retired altogether. Tommy had learned how to fly many years prior to this time and even had a pilot's license at one time, but had been inactive for many years and had never flown a Sky Master. Since I was also a pilot he wanted me to help him get his airplane back in the air and teach him how to fly it. The only problem with that plan was the fact that at that time I did not have a twin rating either so I had to get qualified in the airplane first. By this time Tommy was in his eighties and he and I both knew that he would not live forever so we came up with a plan to help both of us to obtain our goals. Tommy proposed a deal between he and I, that if I would get my twin rating and learn how to fly his plane and then teach him to fly it and get his license up to date that he would sell me the airplane for $5000.00. Part of the deal was also, that if he sold me the plane at that price, that even if he wasn't able to get his license that I would agree to take him flying whenever I flew anywhere provided he was available to go. We had numerous conversations and collaborations on this venture together and eventually I drafted a legal document to close the deal which I have included for the purpose of clarification. I didn't realize it before we started down this road together, but there are a lot of things to consider.

This document is being created in order to record the gentleman's agreement between David Wayne Boudreaux (here-in-after referred to as David) and Thomas James Almond (here-in-after referred to as Tommy) concerning the gift of Tommy's Cessna Sky Master N358 to David. This agreement is being documented for the purpose of eliminating any conflict that could evolve in the future should anything happen to either party. The agreement between David and Tommy is as follows:

1. Any expenses, including parts and labor, hanger rent or any other expenses other than fuel or oil that are acquired by this aircraft after the signing of this agreement will be the responsibility of David. The fuel and oil used by the aircraft will be the responsibility of the person using the aircraft at the time. The main tanks should be filled at the end of each use leaving them full. The aux tanks will only be filled when needed.
2. Should the new owner (David), decide in the future to have this aircraft insured, it will be his sole responsibility to pay the insurance premium.
3. Should any damage be caused to the aircraft during its operation either in the air or on the ground, which is not covered by insurance, the damage to the aircraft or other property will be the sole responsibility of the person operating the aircraft at the time of the incident. Should this incident occur while both parties are in the aircraft acting as pilot and copilot, then both parties will bear responsibility equally.
4. Should an accident occur resulting in the death of any of the aircraft's occupants while Tommy is pilot in command, including Tommy, David Shall not be held for accountability for such deaths, however David will be responsible for the repairs to the aircraft should he decide it is repairable.
5. Should Tommy pass away prior to David the aircraft will become the sole property of David provided he, upon notification and within three

months of said death, surrenders monetary gifts in the amount of $5000.00 to Cynthia Marie Almond, (here-in-after referred to as Cindy).
6. The monies mentioned in the previous statement can be paid at any time that is convenient in the future by David to Cindy, however, if David should decide to sell the aircraft prior to the distribution of the monetary gifts mentioned above, David will notify Tommy or his legal representative of such intent. The balance of the monetary gifts should be surrendered to Cindy within 14 days of the completion of the sell. Any additional funds paid to David during the sell will be his to do what he wants.
7. Should David pass away prior to Tommy the aircraft will become the sole property of Tommy with no exchange of monies and the aircraft should be released to Tommy or his legal representative by David's representative.
8. Should David pass away after he has distributed the gift mentioned above ($5000.00) to Tommy or to Cindy, then the aircraft will be part of David's estate and will be distributed to his survivors per his will.

This should be considered a legally binding document if or when any of the above mentioned scenarios occur and is to be considered effective upon signing by both parties.

_____   _____
Tommy Almond   David Boudreaux

_____
Notary:

So Tommy and I made the deal and we flew all over the country together. I was able to get my twin rating (that is a whole other story) but I will say after that check ride I was sweaty from head to toe and unsure as to whether I had actually passed the test or not. You can ask anyone who has a twin rating, this check ride is a true challenge to your skill and stamina, or at least it was for me. I really loved flying the old Sky Master and I, just like we had agreed, tried to help Tommy get his license current, but by this time Tommy like I previously mentioned, was in his eighties and it was hard for him. He could keep the aircraft flying straight and level once I got him to our cruising altitude, but he was having a lot of trouble with navigation and take-offs and landings. It was also very difficult for him to hear what was being said on the radios. After a while it became apparent to both of us that he would never be able to pass a check ride on this aircraft, but by this time we had become quite comfortable with the existing arrangement and we really enjoyed each other's company anyhow. After Tommy retired there came a time when he got in a financial pinch and he needed his money so I paid him the $5000.00 that I owed him and the plane officially became my property. Let me just say, that I wouldn't suggest making this kind of deal with just anyone. It turned out to be the best thing that could have happened for Tommy and I, but I don't think it would have worked out with anyone else that I know. Incidentally this brings up another topic that happens regularly with aircraft owners, and a subject that we have not covered, and that is aircraft owner partnerships. As we all know aircraft can very expensive for the average person and partnerships can be a viable option for those who want to be an owner, but are not financially able to take on this type of commitment without assistance. Not only are aircraft expensive to purchase, but they can also be very expensive to operate and maintain. This is especially true with a multi-engine aircraft such as the Sky Master. One of the reasons Tommy was willing to let me have the airplane so cheap is because he realized that if he was going to retire he would never be able to afford to keep the aircraft flying. In the few years that he had owned the plane he had spent thousands of dollars trying to keep the aircraft airworthy and never was able to get qualified to fly it. With me being the pilot and the mechanic this way he would be able to still fly when he wanted to and not have the expenses of ownership including costly maintenance and aircraft parts and fuel and oil. This was a perfect solution for his situation, however most partnerships do not start out this way, and do not exactly work this way either.

In a typical aircraft partnership there will be two or more partners (I have seen up to five) in on the purchase of an aircraft. They will generally all contribute equal portions toward the purchase. Sometimes, if one of the partners is an A & P mechanic or an Inspection Authorization (IA), then he or she may be allowed in on the partnership without contributing monetarily by offering his or her services to maintain the aircraft for the partnership. Anyhow, the purchase is only the beginning, after that then it has to be decided how the operating cost and the maintenance expenses will be handled. Normally each partner will contribute equally to the maintenance expenses as well which includes anything that breaks down on the aircraft during the year and an annual inspection at the same time every year. I mentioned earlier that a typical annual inspection on a single engine aircraft is around $2000.00 a year and then on tip of that is about another $2000.00 on parts and labor to repair the items found during the inspection. Again, this is on a single engine aircraft, on a twin engine aircraft you can roughly double that amount. For most people, a twin engine aircraft is too expensive to maintain and operate for a single owner and so a lot of times this is an ideal situation for a partnership. As for the other expenses, it is most often agreed that in a partnership it is a good idea to have the aircraft insured and that opens up a whole new can of worms. Insurance can also be very expensive with the average cost to obtain around $45,000.00 worth of hull coverage with mid time pilots being $5000.00 to $7,000.00 per year depending on the pilot or pilot's qualifications. If the aircraft is to be used for instructional purposes, or for low time pilots, then the insurance cost would be even higher. On top of that if anything breaks down on the aircraft during the year, that is not considered to be a direct result of negligence on the part of one of the partners, then that cost would be divided equally as well. For an aircraft that is flown around 100 hrs per year (average) that cost on a twin can be estimated at $5000.00 per year. Then there is the consideration of engine and propeller overhaul cost that should be calculated in as well. These engines are recommended an overhaul every 2000 hrs time in service (TIS) and so are the propellers. An average engine overhaul is $40,000 and this aircraft has two of them. The average constant speed propeller overhaul is around $14,000.00 and this aircraft has two of them also. That would be a total of $108,000.00 for all of these overhauls every 2000 hours TIS. If the aircraft is at mid life on these overhauls and the plane is flown an average of 100 hrs per year then you would have ten years to have the money set aside for these expenses. These estimated yearly expenses are normally taken care of by a general fund that has been established between the partners where each partner contributes a set amount each month. Of course the purchase price of the aircraft would be an upfront cost and not part of the general fund, but the aircraft will normally already be in an airworthy condition and have a fresh annual inspection so there would be no other upfront cost except the insurance premium for the first year and the cost of the pre-buy inspection/annual. If two partners were involved in purchasing this Sky Master the costs would be around $25,000.00 for the purchase plus $3000.00 for the insurance plus $2000.00 for the pre-buy inspection for a total of $30,000.00 per person. In order to pay the other yearly expenses for the insurance and the annual inspections and estimated maintenance costs and the engine and propeller overhauls, each partner would have to contribute around $1100.00 a month to the general fund in order to pay all of the yearly costs and have the funds needed for overhauls that would be required in ten years if the aircraft is flown 100 hrs per year. In addition to that each partner would be responsible for their own travel expenses such as fuel and oil that would be required to make a trip. Aviation gasoline (Avgas) is between $6.00 and $7.00 per gallon right now depending on where you are located geographically so we will use $6.50 for our estimate. The Sky Master burns around twenty gallons per hour at cruise which is around 185 mph. The aircraft holds 120 gallons of fuel so we will base our estimate on the distance with one full tank of fuel with a half hour of reserve fuel so we have 110 gallons available. That means we can travel for 5.5 hrs at 185 mph which is 1017.5 miles. At $6.50 per gallon we spent $780.00 on fuel. On average these engines will burn around one quart of oil per hour and the oil is around $10.00 per quart. Between the two engines running for 5.5 hrs each that is 6 quarts of oil for the trip at and at $10.00 per quart that is an additional $60.00 in oil. That means that our trip to grandma's house cost us $840.00 just in gas and oil. Look at the bright side though; it probably would have taken us 20 hrs to make this same trip in our car. One of the reasons the aircraft is faster has nothing to do with speed. The highways do not go in straight lines and therefore in this trip across the country following the roads would have been around two hundred miles further in your car.

Those are the disadvantages of flying a twin, but for the person who makes these types of trips often and can afford the cost associated with it, there are several advantages to the twin as well. First let me say that any twin engine aircraft that you operate will cost this much to operate or more. Secondly, any high performance complex aircraft will also have similar operating cost. The annual inspections and the engine and propeller overhaul cost will only be about half the price for single engine high performance aircraft with similar airspeeds, but all the other cost will be close to the same. You may also want to consider this; the twin engine aircraft may cost almost twice as much in fuel, but if you are in a hurry it also goes almost twice as fast as the single engine fixed pitch, fixed landing gear type aircraft that burns half as much fuel. Personally I have found that travelling across the country in a single engine low performance aircraft or in a twin engine high performance complex aircraft cost about the same. The single only burns half as much gas per hour, but it takes almost twice as long to get there. Another factor to consider is how uncomfortable you can get sitting in a small cramped space in a small airplane for five or six hours, then having to stop somewhere for fuel, and then get back in the plane and go another five hours. It is very nice and convenient to be able to make this long of a trip in a roomy comfortable airplane and only have to be in the plane for four or five hours to get where you are going and not have to stop somewhere for fuel. I have also, especially if you are travelling with the family, had to make several stops in my small plane to let everyone go to the restroom. Most twin aircraft are large enough on the inside to be able to make these types of stops unnecessary. In my opinion however, none of these advantages make it worth the extra expense of owning a twin, but this next advantage I'm going to tell you about does. Personally, when I am flying a single engine aircraft I am constantly looking for a place to put the aircraft down in the event of an engine failure. As I have said before, today's aircraft engines are very reliable, but an engine failure is not out of the question. Almost every pilot I know can tell you a story about an emergency landing that they had to make because of an engine failure or a close call. I don't know about you, but that doesn't give me a warm fuzzy feeling when I'm flying. Every pilot is trained on how to deal with an engine failure, and no, it doesn't mean that everyone is going to die, but it does cause one to be constantly aware of the possibility. For me, that means always looking for an emergency landing spot every step of the way. When flying a twin I do not worry so much about an engine failure as when flying a single. When flying a single I do not want to fly over water, I do not want to fly at night and I do not want to fly over clouds because I can't see the ground. I'd rather be on the ground wishing I was in the air than in the air wishing I was on the ground. When I am flying my twin I have peace of mind knowing that if I were to lose an engine all I would need to do is call ahead and tell them I'll be 20 minutes late. Just to be clear, it is still possible to have both engines fail, but that is extremely rare. My peace of mind when flying a twin makes the trip so much more safe and comfortable that it is well worth the extra expense. Before I got my twin I flew my Cessna 172 everywhere and I didn't even realize that I was spending so much time looking for emergency landing spots, but after I started flying my twin I found myself having extra time to do anything I wanted while I was flying because I wasn't so concerned about engine failures.

After I sold my business in Orange Texas in September of 2022 my family and I decided it was the Lord's will for us to sell everything and move to Hood River Oregon. We believe the Lord has led us here because of the way that it all came about, but that is another story for another time. Anyhow, here in Hood River, the company that I now work for, Hood Aero, has brought me here as the Chief of Maintenance at their facility at the Ken Jernstedt Airfield (4S2). Here in Hood River I am responsible for assisting in maintaining the aircraft that belong to Hood Aero and Hood Tech Aero which includes several Cessna 182s and 182 RGs, several piper cubs and super cubs, several Cessna 172s and a couple of Cessna T206H aircraft. I am also responsible for all of the maintenance on the aircraft that do not belong to the company, but are based on the airfield in Hood River and choose to use our facility to maintain their aircraft. In addition to the aircraft that I have already mentioned I have also worked on several other types of pipers such as a PA28-200 Arrow and a PA24-250 Comanche as well as several different models of Mooney aircraft and others. Since the company has not had maintenance personnel available here in Hood River for a long time we are still trying to re-establish a larger customer base. If you live in the Hood River Oregon vicinity, or know someone who does and you or they could use our services, please spread the word. Hood Aero operates a number of aircraft maintenance and fuel and flight training services across the States of Oregon, Washington and Texas. One of those bases is in Dallesport Washington (KDLS) which is about thirty miles east of Hood River Oregon. When my crew does not have an enormous amount of work to do in Hood River we will go to Dallesport to assist the maintenance crew there. One of the projects that we have been working on there is a Cessna O2A (Oscar Deuce) aircraft. This is the military version of the Cessna 337 that I owned and flew all over the country with Tommy and other friends. I have been told that the company purchased this aircraft about four years ago and had one of their pilots fly it to Dallesport where it has been sitting on the ground all this time. They had decided to do a major inspection on the aircraft when it got here and it was determined that the aircraft needed a significant amount of work done to it before it could fly again. They had also purchased this aircraft with a specific mission in mind for how the aircraft was to be utilized by the company and it would require numerous modifications in order to be able to function in this capacity. After this determination had been made the aircraft was disassembled to do the modifications, repairs and upgrades, but it was never finished. I am sure that when I was hired as the Chief of Maintenance in Hood River, the fact that I had owned a 337 for several years and had been the sole maintainer on this aircraft, as well as the pilot, was taken into consideration. I was tasked with the responsibility of finishing the restoration of this O2A as well as the needed modifications to return the aircraft to service and prepare it for the missions that it was purchased for. I believe it is nothing less than miraculous how the good Lord prepared me for this task ahead of time without me even being aware of what was ahead. I have been working on this project for about 4 months now and we are nearing the end. The aircraft is also getting significant avionics upgrades with glass panels and dual digital engine monitoring systems. As it turns out, I was also prepared ahead of time to have the ability and the qualifications to fly this aircraft which no-one else that is based in this area with the company has. As this project comes near its end as for as the maintenance is concerned, I am growing more anxious and excited about the opportunity to be a part of the aircrew that will return this aircraft to service.

You never know where life will take you so you should always be ready, willing and able to learn new things, take advantage of every opportunity, and embark on every new journey with excitement and anticipation. I hope that I have been able to not only provide you with some very valuable information as you pursue your goals in your aviation related activities, but also encourage you to continue down the road of success that you have begun or have imagined. Whether it is, for fun, for a side venture, or for a career, I would encourage you to continue to advance in your aviation endeavors.

Boudreaux's wife Marie walked into de kitchen to see Boudreaux sitting at de table holding a fly-swatter.

So Marie ax Boudreaux, 'mai cher , yu havin any luck wit killin dem dar flies?'

Boudreaux say, 'mai yea, I done kill me two males and tree females already.'

Marie look at Boudreaux funny and say, 'mai how know dem male and female?'

Boudreaux say, 'oh dat easy cher, two of dem was on my beer and tree was on de phone.'

You know, no Boudreaux book could be complete without a few Cajun jokes.

David Boudreaux
Chief of Maintenance
Hood Aero
3624 Airport Dr.
Hood River, OR. 97031

www.ingramcontent.com/pod-product-compliance
Lightning Source LLC
LaVergne TN
LVHW051058100526
838202LV00086BA/6896